COUNTRIES OF THE WORLD

Brazil

Gareth Stevens Publishing
MILWAUKEE

About the Author: Dr. Leslie Jermyn is a professional anthropologist who has done field research in both South and Central America. An experienced teacher, she has written both for academic and popular audiences.

PICTURE CREDITS

A.N.A. Press Agency: 3 (center), 19 (top), 20 (top), 57, 62, 79
Bes Stock: 7 (bottom)
Camera Press Ltd: 84
Bruce Coleman Collection: 7 (top), 9, 13, 40, 47, 89
Contexto: 2, 14 (all), 15 (top), 34, 48 (top), 55, 72 (both), 73 (bottom), 77 (bottom), 78, 80, 81, 83
DDB Stock Photography: 76
Focus Team Photo Agency: 26 (both), 27, 51, 65, 73 (top)
Haga Library Inc.: 12 (top), 46, 68, 87, 91
Jeremy Horner: 8
The Hutchison Library: 21, 36, 54, 58 (top), 66 (bottom)
Björn Klingwall: 16, 31, 32
John Maier, Jr.: 5, 56, 71
Eugene G. Schulz: 41
Pietro Scòzzari: 48 (bottom), 49, 77 (top)
Still Pictures: Cover, 1, 3 (bottom), 4, 17, 18, 19 (bottom), 22, 23, 24, 39, 42, 43, 44, 45, 52, 53, 59 (top), 61, 63
Liba Taylor Photography: 35
Topham Picturepoint: 1, 3 (top), 6, 12 (bottom), 15 (bottom), 20 (bottom), 25, 29, 30, 38, 50, 58 (bottom), 59 (bottom), 64 (both), 66 (top)
Trip Photographic Library: 28, 33, 37, 60, 69, 74, 82, 85
Vision Photo Agency Pte Ltd: 10 (both), 11 (both), 67, 70, 75

Digital Scanning by Superskill Graphics Pte Ltd

Written by
LESLIE JERMYN

Edited by
LIM SUAT HUI AUDREY

Designed by
HASNAH MOHD ESA

Picture research by
SUSAN JANE MANUEL

First published in North America in 1999 by
Gareth Stevens Publishing
1555 North RiverCenter Drive, Suite 201
Milwaukee, Wisconsin 53212 USA

For a free color catalog describing
Gareth Stevens' list of high-quality books
and multimedia programs, call
1-800-542-2595 (USA) or
1-800-461-9120 (CANADA).
Gareth Stevens Publishing's
Fax: (414) 225-0377.
See our catalog, too, on the World Wide Web:
gsinc.com

© **TIMES EDITIONS PTE LTD 1999**
Originated and designed by
Times Books International
an imprint of Times Editions Pte Ltd
Times Centre, 1 New Industrial Road
Singapore 536196
http://www.timesone.com.sg/te

Library of Congress Cataloging-in-Publication Data
Jermyn, Leslie.
Brazil / by Leslie Jermyn.
p. cm. -- (Countries of the world)
Includes bibliographical references and index.
Summary: An overview of Brazil, including an in-depth section on a variety of topics that make the country unique.
ISBN 0-8368-2258-7 (lib. bdg.)
1. Brazil--Juvenile literature. [1. Brazil.] I. Title.
II. Series: Countries of the world (Milwaukee, Wis.)
F2508.5.J47   1998
981--dc21   98-35728

Printed in Singapore

1 2 3 4 5 6 7 8 9 03 02 01 00 99

Contents

5 AN OVERVIEW OF BRAZIL

6   Geography
10 History
16 Government and the Economy
20 People and Lifestyle
28 Language and Literature
30 Arts
34 Leisure and Festivals
40 Food

43 A CLOSER LOOK AT BRAZIL

44 The Amazon Rain Forest: A Treasure
46 The Amazon River
48 Art for the People, By the People
50 Bahia: Soul of Brazil
52 Brazilian Gold: For Better or Worse?
54 Candomblé: Religion of the People
56 Carnival Time in Rio
58 Chico Mendes: A Martyr to the Cause
60 Economic Miracle: Miracle for Whom?
62 Kayapo: Symbols of the Forest
64 Move that Body!
66 Pelé: King of Soccer
68 São Paulo
70 Slavery
72 The Written Word

75 RELATIONS WITH NORTH AMERICA

For More Information ...
86 Full-color map
88 Black-and-white reproducible map
90 Brazil at a Glance
92 Glossary
94 Books, Videos, Web Sites
95 Index

AN OVERVIEW OF BRAZIL

Brazil is truly a giant among nations. It is the largest country in South America and the fifth largest country in the world. It is the only South American country to have been a monarchy, and it was the last to abolish slavery. The nation's varied history and different cultures have contributed to the creation of a uniquely Brazilian society. This book will explore the country's rich variety of people, their music, art, and growing pool of writers. At the same time, it will highlight some of the country's most important problems: the difficulty of preserving natural resources in a poor country, the unequal distribution of wealth in society, and the effect of development on the poor and the uneducated, and on traditional ways of life.

Opposite: **Crowds gather on the beach. Water sports, such as skiing, or just lazing at the beach are extremely popular Brazilian pastimes.**

Below: **A group of Brazilian boys. Brazil has the largest population in South America.**

THE FLAG OF BRAZIL

The Brazilian flag is green with a yellow diamond in the center. Inside the diamond is a blue globe that has a banner across the equator. On the banner are the words "Ordem e Progresso," which means "Order and Progress." Below the scroll are twenty-six five-pointed stars. Each star represents a state. A single star above the banner represents the capital, Brasília. The stars in the blue globe represent the night sky over Rio de Janeiro. The two main colors on the flag, yellow and green, represent Brazil's rich mineral resources, especially gold, and its extensive forests.

Geography

Brazil is the largest country in South America. It covers an area of 3,286,487 square miles (8,512,001 square kilometers), larger than the continental United States, and includes nearly all ecological zones on the continent. At its widest point, Brazil measures nearly 2,700 miles (4,344 km). It borders all but two of the other South American countries and has the Atlantic Ocean on its eastern coast. The population was estimated at 160 million in 1998. The capital city is Brasília.

Below: **Paraíba Valley in northeastern Brazil.**

The country is divided into five geographical regions: northeast, southeast, north, south and central-west. Each region has different natural resources, histories, and land use patterns. A coastal plain along the Atlantic Ocean has been the center of settlement for most of Brazil's history. Inland, there are two large highland plateaus: the Guiana Highlands north of the Amazon River and the Brazilian Highlands south of the Amazon. There are three major river systems: the Amazon in the north, the São Francisco in the east, and the Paraná in the south and west. The Paraná empties into the Atlantic as the Rio Plata.

BAHIA: SOUL OF BRAZIL

Bahia and its capital city, Salvador, were the center of colonial life until the discovery of gold shifted attention and wealth southward to Rio in the eighteenth century.

(A Closer Look, page 50)

The Northeast

The northeast region includes the states of Maranhão, Piauí, Ceará, Rio Grande do Norte, Paraíba, Pernambuco, Alagoas, Sergipe and Bahia, as well as the island Fernando de Noronha. This region covers 18 percent of Brazil's land, has 29 percent of its population, and is the poorest of the five regions. Three types of landscapes cut across all nine states: the coast, the *agreste* (ah-GRAYSH-tay) higher up, and the *sertão* (sayr-TAO), the highlands. Coastal land has the most fertile soil. The elevation of the agreste is higher than that of the coast, and there is less rainfall. The sertão is farthest inland and has been periodically plagued by droughts.

The Southeast

The southeast is the richest region in Brazil. It includes the states of Minas Gerais, Espírito Santo, Rio de Janeiro, and São Paulo. Although this region is only 11 percent of the country's territory, 43 percent of the population lives there. It is highly urbanized, with 88 percent of the people living in cities. The three largest cities are: São Paulo, Rio de Janeiro, and Belo Horizonte. The mountains of Minas Gerais have produced gold, diamonds, iron ore, manganese, and bauxite. Crops, such as coffee, sugarcane, and soybeans, are grown around São Paulo. These products have helped industrial growth in this region.

Above: **A bird's eye view of the rain forest and Amazon river banks in Manaus.**

SÃO PAULO

São Paulo is the third largest city in the world. Fifty percent of all Brazilian industry is concentrated in the suburbs of this huge city, and one million cars are made here every year. São Paulo is also Brazil's most diverse city. Immigrants from Europe, the Middle East, and Asia came here in the first half of the twentieth century to participate in São Paulo's coffee and industrial boom.

(A Closer Look, page 68)

Left: **A panoramic view of Rio de Janeiro. Sugar Loaf Mountain stands in the background.**

The North

The north region covers 46 percent of Brazil's land but has only 7 percent of the population. The states included in this vast northern zone are: Amazonas, Pará, Amapá, Roraima, Acre, Tocantins, and Rondônia. The bulk of the region is dominated by the Amazon river basin, which runs from the Andes in the west to the Atlantic in the east. The area is very sparsely settled, with only two cities of over one million inhabitants: Belém and Manaus. With improved transportation networks, settlers are encroaching on the region's indigenous peoples and its precious natural forest resources.

The South

The south is the smallest region, with only 7 percent of the land but a full 15 percent of the population. It includes the states of Paraná, Santa Catarina, and Rio Grande do Sul, which were largely settled by the most recent wave of European immigrants who came to farm and ranch. The climate is temperate, rather than tropical as in the other regions. There are distinct hot and cold seasons, and snow falls occasionally at high altitudes.

Above: **A rainbow over Iguaçu Falls enhances the beauty of this spectacular sight.**

THE AMAZON RAIN FOREST: A TREASURE

The Amazon rain forest covers a third of the South American continent. With rain and warm weather all year round, the rain forest supports an incredible variety of plants and animals.

(A Closer Look, page 44)

The Central-West

The central-west region includes the states of Goiás, Mato Grosso, and Mato Grosso do Sul, along with the Federal District of Brasília. It covers 18 percent of the land, but is home to only 6 percent of the people. The northern section of the region is covered in forest and is part of the vast Amazon river basin. The southern section is similar to the south region, with subtropical forest, brush, and grassland. The world's largest swamp, called the Pantanal, is in the state of Mato Grosso. This region has both a dry season and a rainy season.

All Creatures Great and Small

Brazil includes almost all of South America's major ecosystems, important exceptions being the high mountains of the Andes and the far south of the continent. Before extensive settlement, it had vast forests, including rain forests, palm forests, mountain forests, and softwood forests. Habitats range from deserts covered in trees, shrubs, and cactus to lush savanna grasslands. The Amazon basin may contain 10 percent of all Earth's plants and animals. Only half the plants and two-thirds of the fish there have been identified, and thousands of insect species are still unnamed.

THE AMAZON RIVER

When the Spanish first discovered this river from the Andes side, they called it the River-Sea because of its enormity. It got the name *Amazon* after an expedition of Spaniards set out to explore the basin in 1540. One of the explorers claimed to have seen tall, fair women warriors who fought with bows and arrows like the fabled women of Greek myth known as the Amazons. So the river and the region were called Amazon.

(A Closer Look, page 46)

Below: **Jaguars fight for territory in the Pantanal.**

History

In the sixteenth century, at the time of first contact between Portuguese and indigenous peoples in what is now known as Brazil, there were two to five million Indians belonging to different groups. The Tupí Indians were the first encountered by the Portuguese, when they established trading posts on the coast. By the middle of the sixteenth century, the Portuguese had established more permanent settlements on sugarcane plantations in the northeast, and the main source of labor was indigenous peoples. However, contact with European diseases and slave raids to the interior wiped out large numbers of Indians.

To provide enough workers for the plantations, Portugal began shipping huge numbers of Africans to its new colony. At first, African labor was mostly used to produce sugar, but when the price of sugar fell, other exports were developed. The first of these was gold. The main gold-producing region in the eighteenth century was Minas Gerais in the southeast. Gold was discovered

Above: **Slaves were brought primarily from West Africa.**

Below: **This illustration depicts slaves being punished on a farm.**

in its rivers in 1695 and was one of the primary exports to Europe until the early nineteenth century. Most gold mining was done by individuals who set off alone into the interior of Minas Gerais to make their fortunes and panned for gold in the rivers. With a shift in population toward the southeast, slaves were also sent there to be miners and domestic servants. Eventually, the rivers were exhausted, and gold prospecting became less profitable.

A third main export of colonial Brazil was coffee from the region around São Paulo. As mining declined, those who had become rich invested their money in coffee plantations. Until 1888, when slavery was abolished, slaves also worked on coffee plantations. All three of Brazil's most important cultures, Indian, African, and European, contributed to the country's economic development and growth.

Politically, Brazil remained a colony of Portugal until 1822. The Portuguese prince regent, Dom João, had moved to Brazil in 1808 when Napoleon took over Portugal. Dom João's son, Pedro I, became ruler of independent Brazil in 1822. Pedro II (the son of Pedro I), and his daughter, Isabel, both ruled Brazil until they were deposed in 1889 by people wanting to establish a republic. Brazil was one of the last countries in South America to become independent from Spanish or Portuguese rule.

Above, left: **Pedro I.**

Above, right: **Pedro I's son, Pedro II.**

SLAVERY

Despite a high degree of mixing, there remains a prejudice against people of color stemming from the stigma of slavery and income level. In general, Black and Indian Brazilians are still the poorest in the country and often experience discrimination in society. Sadly, the slaves who built modern Brazil at the cost of their freedom and their lives are still unrewarded for their contributions and even continue to suffer for them.
(A Closer Look, page 70)

Left: **To signify his intention of modernizing Brazil, Juscelino Kubitschek had a new capital city, Brasília, constructed from scratch in the middle of the country. Here is an example of modern architecture in Brasília.**

From independence to the 1920s, Brazil was run by people who used their wealth and influence to control politicians and elections. During the 1920s, people from other sectors of society started to fight this control in a series of revolts. Finally, in 1930, the military agreed to put the leader of the rebels, Getúlio Vargas, in power. Vargas governed Brazil for fifteen consecutive years until 1945, and then again from 1951 to 1954. He began to industrialize the country. He favored Brazilian-owned industry and did not encourage foreign investment. However, Vargas's successor, Juscelino Kubitschek (1956 to 1960), encouraged investments from foreign countries and companies.

João Goulart, a follower of Vargas, was president from 1960 to 1964. Goulart wanted to promote important social changes, including land reform. He also wanted to limit the amount of money foreign companies could take out of Brazil. This made him unpopular with the Brazilian military and foreign powers. On April 1, 1964, the United States supported a military takeover of the government. This began a military dictatorship that lasted until 1985, although direct presidential elections were not held until 1989.

Below: **Former president, Juscelino Kubitschek.**

Above: Workers in the forestry industry cut timber to make roofs.

Miracle or Mirage?

Until 1973, Brazil's economy grew at a spectacular rate. Three main industries developed: iron ore mining, automobile manufacturing, and power (electricity and alcohol) generation. The first two industries relied on cheap oil and gas. In 1973, however, a rise in oil prices throughout the world resulted in a tremendous recession because Brazil no longer had cheap oil for its factories and cars. The government had to borrow money from other countries, creating a large external debt that remained a major economic problem for many years.

The economic crisis was accompanied by increasing social unrest, along with corruption charges against one political leader after another. In 1993, Fernando Henrique Cardoso, as finance minister, introduced a stabilization program. His "Plan Real" was a major triumph; inflation fell, and Cardoso rode to victory in the next presidential elections.

To deal further with economic difficulties, Brazil has joined Mercosur, a trading group that also includes Argentina, Paraguay, and Uruguay. In 1995, the government also initiated a land reform program to give land to peasants.

BRAZILIAN GOLD: FOR BETTER OR WORSE?

There is a saying in Brazil: "Sugar made Brazil, but gold made it better." This expression refers to the first gold rush in Brazil in the late seventeenth century in what became the states of São Paulo, Rio de Janeiro, and Minas Gerais. A second gold rush began in 1978 in the forests of the north. This time, however, it is not certain that gold is making Brazil better.

(A Closer Look, page 52)

Pedro Álvares Cabral (1467–1520)

Cabral was the leader of the Portuguese expedition that sighted Brazil. He was on his way to India around the tip of Africa when winds blew his ships out into the Atlantic Ocean. On April 22, 1500, the expedition spotted Mount Pascoal, a mountain in Brazil. Cabral put into port at what is now called Porto Seguro and stayed about a week, making contact with local Indians. He then continued his journey to India. Based on his reports, the Portuguese subsequently established a colony in Brazil. Cabral is considered the founder of modern Brazil.

Pedro Álvares Cabral

Henrique Dias (?–1662)

Dias was of African descent and distinguished himself as the leader of a small force that fought against the Dutch when they tried to take over parts of northeast Brazil in the seventeenth century. He served in the army from 1633 to 1654 and was recognized as an excellent tactician. He had to fight racism as well as the Dutch in his army career, but he was awarded a number of honors. In 1656, he traveled to Portugal to meet the king's representatives and was granted the right to free all the slaves that had served in his unit during the war. In his honor, all black militia units formed after his were known as "henriques."

Henrique Dias

José Joaquim da Silva Xavier (1748–1792)

Silva Xavier is commonly known by the nickname "Tiradentes," meaning "Tooth-puller," because he occasionally practiced dentistry. He was also a merchant, a soldier, and a physician. He was one of a group of Brazilian-born men who fought early on for Brazilian independence from Portugal. Tiradentes was captured in the revolt against the Portuguese in 1789, called the Inconfidência Mineira, or Mineira Conspiracy, because it originated in the state of Minas Gerais. He confessed to organizing the plot and was executed for treason. Even though the plot was unsuccessful, Brazilians still recognize Tiradentes as the first Brazilian nationalist in their history. He remains one of Brazil's most famous revolutionaries.

José Joaquim da
Silva Xavier

Princess Isabel (1846–1921)

Isabel was heir to the Brazilian throne after her father, Pedro II. Although she never assumed the throne, she did act as regent during her father's absence from Brazil in 1871, 1876, and 1887. She was an able politician with strong ideas of her own. She is most famous for forcing two antislavery laws into effect. The first, in 1871, freed newborn children of slaves; the second, in 1888, freed all slaves. When the monarchy fell from power in 1889, she was exiled and lived out her life in France.

Above: **Princess Isabel**

Getúlio Vargas (1883–1954)

Vargas served as president of Brazil for eighteen years (1930–1945, 1951–1954). He is still recognized as the prime mover in Brazil's campaign to modernize in the twentieth century. He came to power in 1930 as the leader of a revolutionary force that fought against a small group of professional politicians who controlled Brazil on behalf of the big rural landowners. In 1937, Vargas began a period of dictatorship known as the New State. During this time, he developed the manufacturing industry, expanded health and education programs, and strengthened laws protecting workers. In his second term, as an elected president, he was accused of gross corruption. Vargas never accepted calls for his resignation and chose to commit suicide instead. For better or worse, Vargas was the architect of modern, industrial Brazil.

CHICO MENDES: A MARTYR TO THE CAUSE

Francisco Alves "Chico" Mendes was a rubber-tapper who lived in the Amazon rain forest. On December 22, 1988, he was murdered.
(A Closer Look, page 58)

Left: **Vargas saying his farewells to the pilots fighting against Germany in World War II.**

Government and the Economy

Government

Brazil is divided into twenty-six states plus the Federal District of Brasília. It is a federal republic with an elected president and vice-president and a Congress consisting of an 81-member Senate and a 513-member Chamber of Deputies. An appointed cabinet assists the president. Along with the presidency and Congress, there is a third branch of the national government, the judiciary.

The Senate consists of three representatives from each state and the Federal District. They are elected on a rotating basis for eight-year terms. The Chamber of Deputies is directly elected every four years by proportional representation, which means that the number of deputies depends on the size of the population. The judicial branch of the government includes the Federal Supreme Court at Brasília, composed of eleven judges,

Below: **The Palace of Justice in Brasília.**

Left: **A voter casts his ballot during a national election.**

and a Supreme Court of Justice. All supreme court judges are appointed by the president with the approval of the Senate. There are also regional federal courts, military courts, and labor courts.

Each of the twenty-six states and the Federal District also has a state governor and legislature. They have regional courts and constitutions, but all decisions have to agree with those at the national level. State governments do not control a lot of tax money and do not have much power compared to the national government. Governors and state legislatures are elected directly for four-year terms. State-level elections are held concurrently with presidential elections. The Federal District was established in 1960 at Brasília. Before that, Rio de Janeiro was the capital of the country.

Everyone between the ages of eighteen and seventy is obligated to vote, except illiterates, who may choose to vote or not. Voting is not compulsory for those over seventy or between sixteen and eighteen years of age. In an election held October 3, 1994, Fernando Henrique Cardoso won the presidency with 54.3 percent of the vote. He was inaugurated on January 1, 1995, and his coalition of parties controls 33 seats in the Senate and 182 seats in the Chamber of Deputies.

Above: **Sugarcane workers and their horse cart.**

Natural Resources

From the Andes Mountains in the west to the Atlantic Ocean in the east, Brazil has significant natural resources. The resources Brazil has exploited effectively include metals and gems, hydroelectric power from its many rivers, plantation-style production of sugar, coffee, and cotton, and tropical woods. Brazil's large labor force and consumer market have made it one of the industrial giants in the world today.

Agriculture

In the last twenty years, there has been a shift away from cultivating crops as food for Brazilians toward growing export crops for sale abroad. In 1997, Brazil's biggest export crops were coffee, soybeans, tobacco, and sugar. Oranges are exported in the form of orange juice or concentrated juice. Brazil has an extremely wide range of agricultural products, such as rubber, Brazil nuts, cashews, avocados, citrus fruits, wheat, corn, rice, and soybeans. Apart from these products, Brazil is also an important beef producer.

KAYAPO: SYMBOLS OF THE FOREST

The exploitation of resources does not come without a cost. The traditional way of life of the Kayapo and other Indians has been greatly affected by mining and logging in the rain forests.
(A Closer Look, page 62)

Industry

Brazil has two big industrial sectors: production related to natural resources and agricultural products, and production of goods for internal or external consumption. In the first sector, Brazil converts iron ore into steel and produces hydroelectric power. To a lesser extent today, sugarcane is also used to produce alcohol. In the second sector, Brazil produces mechanized farm equipment, such as tractors, cars, trucks, and airplanes. Some are sold internally and some are exported. The same is true of Brazil's production of small appliances, industrial and agricultural chemicals, clothing, and shoes.

Above: **The gold extraction process in progress.**

Imports and Exports

Brazil's primary imports from other countries are electrical equipment, chemicals, transport equipment, oil, food, wheat, coal, fertilizers, and cast iron. Its primary exports are transport equipment; soya products; machinery; iron and other mined products; leather goods, such as shoes; paper; textiles; meat; coffee; sugar; orange juice; and tobacco. Until 1995, Brazil's largest trading partner for both imports and exports was the United States. Other important trading partners are Argentina, Germany, Japan, and Italy.

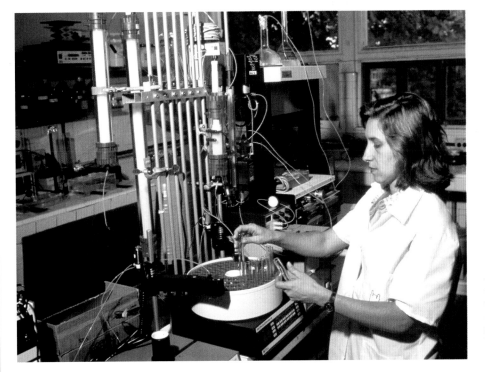

Left: **This woman is conducting research on malaria. There are about sixty-five million workers in Brazil. About one-third are women.**

People and Lifestyle

Ethnicity

Brazil is ethnically quite diverse. The three groups that have contributed to Brazil's population are native Indians, Europeans (primarily Portuguese), and Africans. When the Portuguese first arrived and settled in the northeast, many married Indian women. Their children were called *Mamelucos* (mah-may-LOO-kohs), and they still form the bulk of the population of the sertão in the northeast and of the settlers in the north. When it became clear that Indian slaves could not provide sufficient labor for the sugarcane fields, Africans were forcibly shipped to Brazil in large numbers as laborers. Some of them married Indians, forming a group of descendants called *Cafusos* (cah-FOO-sohs); others mixed with Europeans, creating a larger population of *Mulatos* (moo-LAH-tohs), or mulattoes. In the twentieth century, there has been another wave of immigration bringing large numbers of Europeans, who have settled mostly in the south, and Japanese, who have settled in and around São Paulo.

Above: Amazonian Indians have had to struggle to make their voices heard in the push toward modernization.

Left: Students at an elementary school enjoy their recess.

A Matter of Class

There is a general correspondence between poverty and skin color, so that the richest are definitely the whitest and, conversely, the poorest are black, mulatto, or mixed Indian-European. Facts and figures on poverty in Brazil, the tenth largest industrial economy in the world, are startling. The richest 20 percent earn twenty-six times as much as the poorest 20 percent. The upper class is 10 percent of the population and the middle class is 20 percent, while 70 percent are considered poor.

Rio de Janeiro

In Rio de Janeiro, where there are about fourteen million inhabitants, recent statistics indicate that about two thousand children live permanently on the streets. Other children actually have homes in shantytowns but head out to the streets to either beg or pick pockets. Although they may stay away from their homes for several days, these children still have families consisting of a few siblings and, in most cases, an unmarried mother. The money they obtain helps support the family.

Above: **Children in Olinda, Pernambuco. Brazil's regions can be distinguished by their ethnic composition. For example, the northeast coast has the greatest number of blacks and mulattoes, while the sertão is settled by people of Indian-European descent. The south is almost entirely European, having been settled by the last wave of immigrants from that continent.**

Above: Schoolchildren wait for their class to begin.

Education

Throughout the twentieth century, federal policy has shifted back and forth between making it mandatory for governments to spend a certain proportion on education and ignoring education as a necessary social service. As a result, the system continues to be under-funded and still discriminates against the poor.

Primary education to the eighth grade is obligatory, but few of the really poor can afford this luxury — children are needed to work. Few rural areas even have schools offering all eight grades, and in the poorest areas of the northeast, even the teachers have not completed primary school. Secondary schools are geared toward the elite and middle classes and are well beyond the reach of the poor. Universities are public but not really accessible to the poor because they cannot get through primary and secondary levels. For the few who obtain post-secondary education but have to work to support themselves or their families, free university is impossible because classes are offered only during the day. Night classes are available only in private institutions that charge tuition fees. Two-thirds of the education budget devoted to universities subsidizes the rich or middle-class students who can afford to attend day classes.

THE WRITTEN WORD

English readers in Europe and North America are now beginning to appreciate the great works of Latin America. The old pattern of New World writers copying Europeans has been replaced by mutual respect and influence. Despite high levels of illiteracy in Brazil, the country has produced some renowned writers.

(A Closer Look, page 72)

Health

The public health care system in Brazil suffers from the same problems as education: lack of money and unequal regional distribution of services. The rich have access to and can afford up-to-date hospitals and clinics, while the poor are lucky to get emergency care. Regionally, the northeast is again disadvantaged, with only about one-third of households receiving piped-in water and only one in six having sewage systems. Unclean water and living conditions are big contributors to infant mortality, which is twice as high in the northeast as the southeast. The national average life expectancy is only sixty-six years.

The issues of poverty, education, and health are related. It is the poor who lack schooling and public health care and, as a result, cannot compete for work. So they stay poor into the next generation. If Brazil wants to help its poor, it will have to change both its education and health care systems.

ECONOMIC MIRACLE: MIRACLE FOR WHOM?

Despite the country's "economic miracle" for many years, those who have suffered the most are poor women and children. Working women are paid the least and are usually the first to lose their jobs when there are layoffs. Children suffer from a lack of social services and education.

(A Closer Look, page 60)

Left: **Although there is still hunger in Brazil, food prices are definitely less of a burden today than in the past, and the poor are able to feed themselves.**

All in the Family

The extended family, including grandparents, aunts, uncles, cousins, and in-laws, is considered a person's most valuable resource. Brazilians count on their families for help with money or other problems. Middle- and upper-class Brazilians, especially, maintain extensive family ties and may even share living space with their elderly parents or married children. Even when staying in retirement homes, the elderly are frequently visited by their family members. When young married people set up a new household, they will usually choose somewhere close to one or both sets of parents. Extended families that do not live together generally try to have Sunday lunch together.

Below: **A large family in Brazil. Brazilians rely on their families for help with money or problems.**

There are two ways large families become even larger: godparenthood and informal adoption. At the birth of a child, the parents will ask two other adults to become the child's godparents. These people assume some of the responsibility for the child and may help with education expenses if they can. Wealthy people will also sometimes "adopt" poorer, distant relatives or the children of workers or servants. These children are not officially adopted, but they will move in with the richer employer or relatives and receive economic help from them.

Children Should Be Heard and Seen

Children accompany adults on all social visits, unless it is very late. They are not kept apart from adults and learn early on how to interact appropriately in adult situations. From a young age, children learn strong family ties. They are not encouraged to be overly independent and will usually share sleeping space with siblings of the same sex. Even when grown up, they stay at home as long as possible, leaving only when they are married. Even then, if young couples living in an urban area cannot afford a place of their own, they will stay with one set of parents or the other. The many benefits of making this choice include paid bills, ready meals, and savings on home rental.

Women's and Men's Roles

Brazilian boys and girls are raised with different expectations. Girls and women are expected to stay home and look after their families. Men are considered the heads of households and are usually responsible for providing for the family. Forty percent of married women work but usually not in high-paying or executive jobs. Many families may also have a woman as the breadwinner. Both urban and rural women have a major say in the way their family is run.

Above: **Brazilian children in a group pose. Brazilian boys and girls face different expectations.**

CANDOMBLÉ: RELIGION OF THE PEOPLE

Candomblé is practiced mostly by people of African descent in the northeastern region of the country. The slaves who worked on the sugar plantations of this region brought their religious beliefs with them and continued to practice them in Brazil. The Portuguese slave owners forced the slaves to convert to Catholicism and forbade the practice of African religion. To be able to worship their own gods and saints, the slaves blended them with Catholic symbols.
(A Closer Look, page 54)

Left: People gathered for a religious ceremony in Bahia. Religion in Brazil is incredibly diverse. This diversity is one of the key defining characteristics of Brazilian society as a whole.

Religion

The vast majority of Brazilians are Catholics, and Brazil has the largest population of Catholics in the world today. However, Brazilians also believe in supernatural forces other than those accepted by the Catholic Church. One source of modern Brazilian religious practice is the African religions brought over by slaves. Brazilian slaves came mostly from West Africa and Angola, and the religions of these people are still recognizable in Brazilian cults such as *candomblé* (cahn-DOM-blay) and *umbanda* (oom-BAN-dah). The beliefs of members of candomblé and umbanda show very clearly how African and Catholic systems have combined to make something distinctly Brazilian. For example, the African goddess of the sea, Iemanjá, is believed to be the same as the Virgin Mary, the mother of Jesus.

Below: Religious icons of the Catholic faith.

Other Beliefs

Other beliefs are no longer practiced to the same degree as candomblé and umbanda. One example is the belief in *carrancas* (kahr-RAN-kahs), which were carvings of monsters specially designed to fit on the front of boats. The monsters were believed to frighten away any evil spirits living in the water and waiting to sink ships. Today, boats do not have carrancas, but fishermen will still paint eyes on their boats to "see" the dangers under the water.

Valley of the Dawn

Newer forms of mysticism are springing up all the time. One cult, known as the Valley of the Dawn, believes that many people will die at the end of the twentieth century, but cult members will be saved. They built a large temple about 35 miles (56 km) from Brasília and filled it with new gods and goddesses drawn from Indian, African, and Catholic traditions. The village around the temple has a school, a hotel, two restaurants, and an ice-cream parlor. Believers live much like other rural Brazilians.

Below: A candomblé ceremony in progress at a beach.

Language and Literature

Express Yourself!

The official language, and the one spoken by most Brazilians, is Portuguese. Brazilian Portuguese is different from the Portuguese spoken in Portugal. When the first settlers from Portugal arrived, they spoke a type of Portuguese common in the seventeenth and eighteenth centuries. In the nineteenth century, the king of Portugal transferred his empire to Brazil, bringing European influence to the language. Since then, however, Brazilian Portuguese has been fairly isolated from European forms and has developed on its own. Brazilian Portuguese also picked up new words from both the indigenous Tupí-Guaraní peoples and African slaves. Within Brazil itself, there are differences in how Portuguese is spoken. There are different regionalisms and accents. For example, *carioca* (kahr-ree-OH-ka) refers to people born in Rio and their accent.

Left: **A Brazilian boy reads a Portuguese book. Portuguese is a romance language, which means it was heavily influenced by Latin under the Roman Empire in Europe.**

Cordels and More

Brazilian fiction is characterized by its concern with a certain set of Brazilian themes: Indian people, African slaves and their modern descendants, drought, the sertão or backlands, the Amazon jungle and river, Bahia, and modern mega-cities like São Paulo and Rio. However, popular kinds of writing, such as comic books and local songs, also reflect important themes in people's lives. These are usually not distributed outside the area where they are published and, therefore, are not widely known.

One such form of writing in Brazil is the *cordel* (COR-dayl) of the northeast. Cordel means "cord" and refers to the way these pamphlets are sold strung up on strings in stalls. They are usually a few pages long and tell of local events and heroes. Cordels have been most successful in the northeast sertão region where land is controlled by rich bosses, poor landless people struggle to make a living, and drought is a constant threat to livelihood. Although many people in the sertão region are illiterate, they still enjoy cordels because this literature is also performed by singers who specialize in this form of work.

Opposite: **Examples of advertisements in Brazil.**

Arts

Shapes and Sizes

Brazil's first sculptor was Aleijadinho. His religious figures, which were carved in wood and painted, are avidly collected today. Other talented sculptors include GTO (Geraldo Teles de Oliveira), who carves intricate circles of wood filled to overflowing with tiny human figures, and Mário Cravo, who works in a more modern medium, using concrete to create his abstract shapes.

Left: **This sculpture, entitled "Two Warriors," stands in Brasília.**

MOVE THAT BODY!

Samba and bossa nova music from Brazil are both world famous. *Samba* (SAM-bah) has evolved into distinct forms. Some, such as the *samba-canção* (SAM-bah Kahn-SOW), are slower with an emphasis on melody, while others, such as *samba de roda* (SAM-bah day ROH-dah), emphasize percussion and are accompanied by hand-clapping.
(A Closer Look, page 64)

Tale of a Brazilian Composer

One of the most famous Brazilian classical music composers was Heitor Villa-Lobos (1887–1959). Born in Rio, Villa-Lobos learned how to play the cello from his father, who was a library official and an amateur musician. Villa-Lobos never received any formal musical training but was passionate about music from an early age. He gave his first public show in 1915. In 1927, he performed in Paris, which established him as an international composer. Villa-Lobos's music features a lot of percussion, as does most popular and traditional Brazilian music. He is easily Latin America's most famous twentieth century composer.

Theater

Until World War II, Brazilian playwrights generally wrote pure entertainment for the elites of the big cities. Beginning in the 1940s, European exiles from the war started changing Brazilian theater, both in terms of staging techniques and in terms of the plays written. Many smaller theater groups emerged at this time, and plays began to deal with important social issues, such as the differences between rich and poor and, later, after 1964, torture and repression under the military. Today, Brazilian theater is experimental and original, and has dealt with changing technology by producing plays for television audiences.

Above: **The opera house shown here is located in Manaus. Rio got its first theater, Teatro Real de São João, in 1808 when the Portuguese crown relocated to Brazil. The oldest theater in Brazil is in Ouro Preto in Minas Gerais and dates back to the early eighteenth century.**

Architectural Flair

During the colonial period, Jesuit missionaries brought the Baroque style of architecture to Brazil. Churches were built in this style, which is very ornate with many carvings and fluid lines decorating the building. The style originated in Europe, but as Indian and locally born craftsmen gained influence over their craft, the carved faces came to be more Indian-looking than European. In the eighteenth century, as the economy shifted south to Rio and Minas Gerais, so too did Baroque influence on architecture. In Ouro Preto in Minas Gerais, money from gold mining sponsored many public and religious buildings.

The next big movement in Brazilian architecture was the building of the new capital city, Brasília. In 1956, two Brazilian architects, Lúcio Costa and his student, Oscar Niemeyer, were awarded the job of designing a modern capital city. Brasília was the architectural wonder of Latin America when it was built because it was a modern city built completely from scratch in a semi-arid region. The presidential palace, Itamaraty Palace, and Brasilia's cathedral both demonstrate Costa's and Niemeyer's vision of open spaces and curving lines.

Above: Brasilia's cathedral, an example of clean geometric lines and shapes. Critics say Brasília looked better on paper than when it was actually constructed because the buildings were too big to be harmonious. Yet, Brasília still stands as an incredible architectural wonder.

Arts and Crafts

Various regions in Brazil are known for their crafts. Minas Gerais produces beautiful soapstone carvings and useful objects, such as bookends and ashtrays, from quartz and agate. The northern Amazon region is known for its Indian handicrafts. The Indians use natural materials to make jewelry; weapons, such as bows and arrows; and musical instruments. One instrument, the rainstick, became quite popular in North America. It is a hollow, wooden tube with seeds inside. When the tube is turned on end, the seeds moving through it sound like falling rain.

Precious woods are made into many different objects. Some, such as bowls, are functional, and some are decorative. The northeastern region produces beautiful embroidered cotton clothing and lace. Ceramic jugs and cooking utensils are also made in the northeast, where food is often prepared in this type of vessel. A special type of pottery called *marajoara* (mah-rah-joh-AHR-ah) comes from the island of Marajó at the mouth of the Amazon River.

ART FOR THE PEOPLE, BY THE PEOPLE

Brazilian artists have produced works of distinction. At a show in 1946, Eleanor Roosevelt saw the paintings of Djanira da Mota e Silva and wrote a very positive review in her daily newspaper column. After that, Djanira's work received recognition both abroad and back home in Brazil.
(A Closer Look, page 48)

Below: Beautiful soapstone carvings with intricate designs.

Leisure and Festivals

Leisure

Major Brazilian cities have clubs for tennis, fitness, and other sports. World class cities, such as Rio and São Paulo, have extensive shopping areas for those with money to spend. For evening entertainment, restaurants, clubs, theaters, and cinemas are available. With one of the longest coastlines in the world, water activities, such as sailing, swimming, and diving, are popular. For the average Brazilian, however, with limited time and money, leisure activities are much simpler and cheaper.

Left: **Many Brazilians have fun in the sun, but it is a luxury the average Brazilian cannot afford.**

Watching the Goggle Box

Many Brazilian families spend evenings in front of the television. The most popular type of show is the *telenovela* (tay-lay-noh-VAY-lah), an evening soap opera. A large percentage of the population will follow one or another of these shows for as long as it lasts, and that can be up to ten months. Another popular television program is *Jornal Nacional*, a news show, which began in 1968. Today, about 60 percent of the viewing population see it every night. That means about thirty-five million people tune in!

Speak Your Mind

Besides organized events or programs, Brazilians also appreciate the fine art of conversation. They will often pass their leisure hours talking to friends and neighbors at home or in a local café or bar. These conversations are often informal affairs, where people just happen to meet somewhere and take advantage of the opportunity to have a chat. Brazilians are known to be experts at "small talk," and they also enjoy political arguments and debates.

Above: **Brazilians enjoying a picnic. Sundays are a day of rest for most Brazilians. They often spend the day with family, and the focus is the midday meal.**

Soccer

Soccer is more than just a sport for Brazilians — it is a passion. Every neighborhood and village has some sort of soccer field and soccer ball. The poorest and most isolated communities will use coconuts, if necessary, to be able to play the national sport. Big cities, such as Rio and São Paulo, have enormous stadiums to accommodate their passionate fans. Brazilians enjoy soccer in two ways: as participants and as spectators. Most Brazilian boys start playing the game when they are very young, and a friendly soccer match between children or adults can happen anywhere, anytime. Brazilians are also avid fans of favorite local teams. Soccer teams or clubs encourage people to become members, and ticket prices for professional games are kept quite low to allow the maximum number of people to attend.

Brazil's national team is known to be one of the best in the world. Individual players, such as Pelé, have become international superstars. Brazil is the only country to have won the World Cup four times: 1958, 1962, 1970, and 1994. Apart from World Cup games, professional soccer is played all year long.

Above: **When important soccer matches take place, businesses often just close up rather than try to operate with no workers. Everyone is at home or at a café watching the game. Crowds of people also fill the stadium to watch the game.**

PELÉ: KING OF SOCCER

Over the course of Pelé's professional career, he scored more than 1,300 goals! This number is particularly impressive because no other player has even reached 1,000!

(A Closer Look, page 66)

Kick It

One sport unique to Brazil is *capoeira* (kah-poh-EYR-ah), a type of musical kickboxing. This martial art may have its origins in a form of fighting brought over by slaves from Angola. It was developed by slaves who were prohibited from any form of fighting. Capoeira is performed to music and looks as much like dancing as fighting. Thus, the slaves were able to fight without their masters knowing what they were doing. Modern capoeira clubs exist all over Brazil, but Rio and Salvador are considered the centers of this sport.

On the International Circuit

Brazilians have also made their mark in other international sports. Three Brazilians have been world auto racing champions: Emerson Fittipaldi, Nelson Piquet, and Ayrton Senna. Maria Bueno is one of the best-known female sports figures. She won tennis championships at Wimbledon and in the United States. Volleyball and basketball are popular, too, and Brazil supports high-quality teams for international competitions, such as the Olympics and the Pan-American Games.

Below: **Two teenagers hone their capoeira skills, while spectators cheer them on.**

Tiradentes Day

Silva Xavier, or Tiradentes, was the first Brazilian to fight for independence from European control in the Mineira Conspiracy. Executed in 1792, he is now celebrated as a martyr. Tiradentes Day is celebrated on April 21, with musical performances and athletic competitions.

Independence Day

Brazil celebrates Independence Day on September 7. On this date in 1822, Pedro de Alcântara (Pedro I) issued the "Cry of Ipiranga," a declaration that Brazil was an empire separate from Portugal.

CARNIVAL TIME IN RIO

Carnival, a Catholic festival, is celebrated before Lent. It features a large parade by different samba schools. The schools save all year long to buy their Carnival costumes!
(*A Closer Look, page 56*)

Left: **Two smart-looking boys on Independence Day. Military parades and floats covered with flowers celebrate the event.**

Religious Festivals

Religious festivals include New Year's Day, Círio de Nazaré, and Christmas. January 1, New Year's Day, is celebrated in Salvador with a procession of small boats, decorated with flags, carrying the statue of Lord Jesus of Seafarers from Todos os Santos harbor to a beach called Boa Viagem. Sailors believe that if they participate in the procession, they will never drown. Círio de Nazaré honors Our Lady of Nazareth. During a procession, the image is pulled on a float by a long rope. People believe that if they touch the rope, their wishes will be granted. The procession is accompanied by thousands of candles.

Below: **Small boats filled with flowers as offerings to the goddess Iemanjá are set afloat at the beach. Many people believe that if a wish is made and the boat floats out to sea, then the wish will be granted by Iemanjá, Queen of the Seas. If the boat returns, the wish is rejected.**

Last, but not least, is Christmas. German immigrants brought many European Christmas traditions with them during the early twentieth century. Children believe in Santa Claus, whom they call *Papai Noel* (PAH-pay NO-ayl). Instead of a Christmas tree, most families have a Nativity scene on display.

Food

A Feast for the Eyes (and Tummy, Too!)

Brazil has many regional food specialties, but there are some foods common to most Brazilian households. The national dish is called *feijoada* (fay-zhoh-AH-dah). The basis of the dish is a stew of black beans and a variety of salted and dried meats such as pork, beef, tongue, sausage, and bacon. The beans and meat are stewed together with onions, garlic, and bay leaves for hours. To accompany the meat and beans, white rice and fried kale are served along with fried manioc flour and fresh orange slices.

Brazil produces its own beer, wine, and spirits. The most popular alcohol is *cachaça* (kah-CHAH-sah), made from sugarcane juice. The national drink is *caipirinha* (kye-peer-EEN-yah), which is cachaça with crushed lime and sugar. Caipirinha is a popular accompaniment to feijoada.

Below: This man is toasting manioc flour. Rice, beans, and manioc are staple foods. Other common items include cooked bananas, squash, and Portuguese dried codfish known as *bacalhau* (bah-kahl-YOW).

Meal Patterns

Brazilians start their day with a small breakfast consisting of coffee with milk, bread, and fresh fruit. Lunch is the biggest meal of the day and, whenever possible, Brazilians try to eat it at home with their families. Many businesses close for two hours at lunchtime to allow people to get home, then stay open an hour later in the afternoon. Some people also eat a small snack with juice or coffee in the afternoon. The evening meal is eaten at home between 7 p.m. and 9 p.m. The most important meal of the week is the Sunday family lunch. It is a chance for the family to catch up with the week's news.

Good Manners

In Brazil, good table manners are indicative of good education and social class. Brazilians generally do not touch their food with their fingers. Pizza, chicken, and even sandwiches are usually eaten with a knife and fork or with a napkin covering the part of the food held in the hand. When Brazilians are having a meal, and another person approaches, they will always offer to share the meal, no matter how small the portion. Finally, they do not like to eat while moving around. Even the smallest snack bars have areas to stand or sit while eating.

Above: **A Brazilian family shares dinner. For snacks, Brazilians enjoy *salgadinhos* (sahl-gah-DEEN-yohs), which are small pastries filled with cheese, ham, shrimp, chicken, or beef. Desserts include a variety of puddings, custards, mousses, and sherbets made with passion fruit and avocado.**

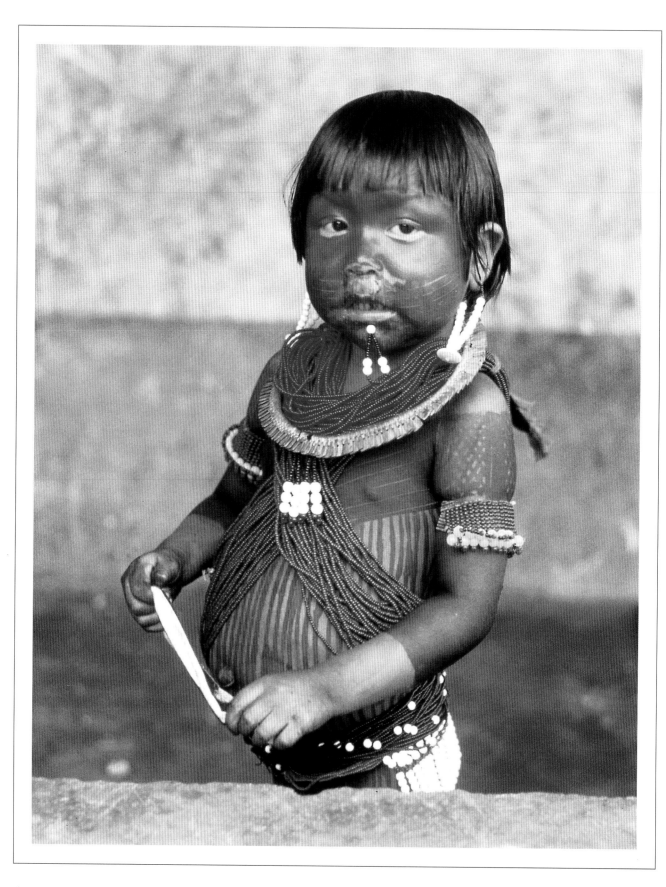

A CLOSER LOOK AT BRAZIL

If you have never heard of the Carnival in Rio, now is the time. It is the most famous Carnival in the world! The following pages also describe other unique aspects of Brazilian life, such as candomblé beliefs, Bahian lifestyle, and the country's incredible landscape. The Amazon River is the second largest in the world; the Amazon rain forest is the largest. These impressive resources are used by diverse wildlife and by many people. Groups who depend on the rain forest include forest Indians, rubber-tappers, and gold miners. Their stories will demonstrate that preserving the Amazon is no easy task.

Opposite: **A young Kayapo child gazes into the camera. To read about the plight of the Kayapo people, turn to page 62.**

Many Brazilians have become famous outside Brazil, whether in sports, music, art, or literature. Pelé, the legendary soccer star, is a familiar figure to soccer fans throughout the world. For others, Jorge Amado's translated books are a pleasure. The country's artists, many of them women, have also made their mark, and a style known as primitive art has caught on. Finally, not only Brazilians dance to the rhythms of Brazil as captured in samba and bossa nova music!

Above: **A boy on a canopy walkway admires the view of a rain forest reserve in the Amazon.**

The Amazon Rain Forest: A Treasure

The Amazon rain forest is the world's largest, covering one-third of South America. It is estimated to contain forty thousand species of plants. Over three thousand kinds of trees thrive there, as well as vines that grow up the trees and plants that grow high on the trees near the sunlight. The latter have no roots and take moisture from the air. There are 1,500 kinds of birds in the Amazon, including parakeets, parrots, and toucans, and 2,500 kinds of fish. Snakes also live in the trees. Some mammals are specially adapted to life in the trees and have prehensile tails to help them move around. One-tenth of all plant and animal species on Earth live in the Amazon rain forest.

Left: The Amazon rain forest has many species of trees. The tallest trees are known as emergents and rise above the rest of the canopy.

Key to the Treasure

Many experts think the best way to preserve the forest is to use it wisely. Rather than prevent Brazilians from profiting from their forest, they should be encouraged to manage the forest and its resources. For example, it is not profitable in the long term or ecologically sound to cut down huge patches of forest for cattle ranching or farming. The soil is very poor and will only support farming or ranching for a few years before no more crops or grass will grow. It is not certain that the forest can grow back once the soil is depleted. A wiser approach is to harvest products that can be sold without destroying the whole forest. Some of these products include Brazil nuts, mahogany trees and other valuable hardwoods, rubber, and medicinal plants. The best source of information about which plants are useful is the indigenous people, so their survival is also essential.

Above: **The destruction of the Amazon rain forest to clear land for cattle ranches has had disastrous consequences.**

The Amazon River

The Amazon River is the second longest in the world; only the Nile is longer. It runs from Lake Lauricocha in the Andes Mountains near the Pacific Ocean to the Atlantic Ocean in the east — a journey of 3,915 miles (6,300 km).

The river was "born" two million years ago when a vast inland sea burst its banks to course across the continent to the Atlantic. Today, the river is fed by a thousand tributaries; many are big enough to be major rivers. The Amazon flows between the two highland plateaus: Guiana in the north and Brazilian to the south. It starts at an altitude of 18,000 feet (5,500 m) above sea level, drops rapidly to the lowlands, and then loses only 2 inches (5 cm) per mile for the next 3,500 miles (5,600 km).

Left: **The Amazon River is so big that 209,280 cubic yards (160,000 cubic meters) of fresh water are emptied into the Atlantic each second! One day's worth of water from the mouth of the Amazon could supply all U.S. homes with water for five full months! The Amazon contributes about 15 percent of the fresh water emptied into the oceans all over the world.**

It is hard to imagine the size and importance of the Amazon, but here are some facts. At the point where the Amazon pours into the ocean, it is 200 miles (322 km) across. At points upstream, it is more than 15 miles (24 km) wide, which means you often cannot see the other shore. It can be up to 250 feet (76 m) deep, which makes it the deepest river in the world.

Indigenous people have lived along the river and its tributaries for millennia. They have depended on the river's periodic flooding to fertilize the land with silt and have used the river as their main form of transportation. Since colonial times, the river has been the main transportation artery into the vast jungle interior. Transport ships carry cargo up the river, and many passenger ships and small *gaiolas* (gay-OHL-ahs) ply the Amazon. These smaller boats are the usual form of transportation for most of the Amazon's inhabitants.

Above: **Fishermen sell their catch on the banks of the Amazon River.**

Art for the People, By the People

Today, many Brazilian painters receive international recognition for their individual yet distinctly Brazilian styles. One popular type of art is "primitive" or "popular" art. Such art is created by someone with no formal training. Primitive art was recognized as art only after Modern Art Week took place in São Paulo in 1922. Painters, poets, writers, and musicians gathered to protest the artistic community's standard tendency to copy European styles and forms. They wanted to show that Brazilians had a distinctive artistic style that was as good as European art and writing. Following Modern Art Week, museums and galleries started featuring the works of untrained Brazilian painters such as Heitor dos Prazeres and José Antônio da Silva. Throughout the twentieth century, many other primitive artists have emerged, many of them women.

Above: **An invitation to Modern Art Week.**

Heitor dos Prazeres

Heitor dos Prazeres was of African descent and grew up in Rio's slums. His paintings are reflections of street scenes and figures common in Rio in the early and middle part of the twentieth century. Besides painting, he composed samba music and wrote poetry. His work was finally given national recognition when he was awarded a prize at the São Paulo Bienal (an art festival) in 1951.

Opposite and *above:* **Examples of Brazilian art. Note the bright, vibrant colors.**

Women in Art

Well-known women artists in Brazil include Wilma, who paints scenes from candomblé rituals; Maria Lacerda, who portrays crowded scenes of Rio life; Isabel de Jesús, who paints magical pictures of flowers, birds, and human figures all intertwined; and Maria Auxiliadora Silva, who perfected a technique to give her pictures depth by adding paste under the paint. All of these women have made important contributions to Brazilian culture and art in general.

Bahia: Soul of Brazil

Bahia was settled by Portuguese sugar plantation owners during the earliest years of the colony, but it was the large number of African slaves brought in to work the estates that made Bahia what it is today. Bahia has Brazil's largest concentration of people of African descent. Seventy percent of Bahians are either black or mulatto. The blending of African, European, and Indian blood that characterizes Brazil in general is nowhere more evident than in Bahia, which is why Brazilians call the area the Soul of Brazil.

The pattern established during the colonial period of a small elite controlling the land and wealth, while the African and Indian majority lived in devastating poverty, unfortunately continues to the present. After a decline in the economic importance of sugar and the end of slavery, a rich elite continued to control agricultural production, and those who had been slaves continued to exist on meager wages. The ongoing economic crisis in this region has created a huge migration from the countryside to the cities. Nevertheless, Brazilian art, music, and literature continue to be dominated by Bahians.

Below: **A market scene in Bahia.**

Food for the Soul

Bahia's cuisine, like everything else there, is a blend of African and Portuguese traditions. The key ingredients are unrefined palm oil, called *dendê* (dayn-DAY) oil, coconut oil, *malagueta* (mah-lah-GAY-tah) chili peppers, okra, and seafood. Bahian women, or *Baianas* (bye-AHN-ahs), make local favorites to sell from street-side or beach-side stands. A regional specialty is *moqueca* (moh-KAY-kah), which is a kind of stew containing shrimp or other seafood, coconut, garlic, onions, parsley, peppers, dendê oil, and tomato paste all simmered together and served with rice cooked in coconut milk. Bahian desserts are also famous throughout Brazil. They are usually made from eggs, coconut, milk, and sugar. *Cocada* (ko-KAH-dah) is a coconut candy boiled in sugar water and flavored with lemon or ginger. Despite its poverty, Bahia is definitely the soul of Brazilian culture.

Above: Selling food near the street. Some of Bahian women's specialties include the *acarajé* (ah-cahr-AH-zhay), or Bahian hamburger. It is not made from meat but from a type of bean mashed up with ground shrimp and onion and then deep fried in dendê oil and served with chilies.

Brazilian Gold: For Better or Worse?

The first gold rush in Brazil was in the late seventeenth century. Interest in Brazilian gold was revived in the 1960s when the military government made a geological survey and discovered that huge river basins of the northwestern forests were likely spots for gold. The modern gold rush began in 1978 when world gold prices rose to new heights. About one million miners headed off into the jungle to find the elusive metal. This gold rush has had disastrous consequences for all concerned because of the methods used and lack of controls on mining operations.

Gold in the north is mined by being dug out of the ground near rivers. The gold is embedded in river sediment and has to be separated from the sediment by the use of mercury. After the sediment is removed, the remaining compound of gold and mercury is burned to remove the mercury as vapor, leaving pure gold.

Below: **The relentless pursuit of gold. For every pound (0.45 kg) of gold produced, 4 pounds (1.8 kg) of mercury are used and eventually released into the forest's water and air systems.**

Left: **The miners, who are poor Brazilians driven to gold mining by desperation, are themselves showing signs of mercury poisoning. They also take huge risks climbing in and out of the mud pits with no safety precautions. Mudslides can kill them with no warning. Given the human and environmental cost of gold, the statement that "gold made Brazil better" seems untrue.**

The Cost of Gold

As a result of these mining techniques, mercury enters both the river systems and the air. Besides affecting the miners, it has also affected indigenous peoples who can no longer fish near their homes because the river is polluted. The river sediment that has been mixed with mercury is eventually washed back into the river, which makes the water murky, killing off plants dependent on light and fish dependent on the plants. Mercury is also highly toxic for all living things. It kills off wildlife, and mercury poisoning in humans causes brain damage, birth defects, and in high enough concentrations, death.

Candomblé: Religion of the People

Candomblé is a kind of religion followed primarily by people of African descent in northeastern Brazil. West African and Catholic beliefs have both contributed to the religion. Candomblé followers believe there should be harmony and balance between humans and the forces of nature. Humans and nature are both the products of Olodumare, the supreme God, and all contain *axé* (AH-shay), or divine energy. The types of energy contained in a person or natural phenomena such as thunder, determine the nature of the personality or aspect of nature. *Orixás* (oh-REE-shahs), or spirits, have particular elements of axé and Olodumare's character.

Candomblé believers think orixás are the intermediaries between humans and God. Candomblé priests communicate with the orixás when they become possessed, or taken over, by these spirits. When the priests are possessed, the orixás can help other people with their problems and illnesses by giving them advice.

Left: **A candomblé dancer in Bahia. People who wish to become part of candomblé train for a long time to learn how to communicate with the orixás. Those who have been members for the longest time have seniority and are respected by junior members.**

A Means of Solidarity

Socially, candomblé is a basis for solidarity. A group of believers in a given area is divided into houses or subsections led by the most senior practitioner, usually a woman. She is known as the spiritual mother and is responsible for the well-being of all her house members. A candomblé house is a group of people who all share the same belief system but who also help one another in times of economic need. Candomblé was once a way for slaves to band together to help one another, and this economic function survives into modern times. Prohibited under colonial rule, candomblé can now be freely practiced, but not everyone in Brazil is a participant.

The Bonfim Festival

Candomblé is still practiced mostly in the northeast where the largest concentration of slaves lived during the colonial period. The Bonfim Festival in Salvador, the capital of Bahia, is a combination of Catholic and candomblé elements. In 1875, a Portuguese ship captain was shipwrecked off the coast of Bahia. While he and his men were floundering in the ocean, he promised God that, if he survived, he would build a church. He did survive and built a church called Our Lord of the Happy Ending (*Bonfim* means "happy ending"). The festival is celebrated every January.

Above: A Bonfim procession. During the week-long festival in January, women followers of candomblé wear their traditional white dresses and participate in parades and processions to the church. On the last day of the Bonfim Festival, they bring jars of water to wash the steps of the church. During the celebrations, they may go into trances as their orixás take possession of them.

Carnival Time in Rio

Carnival is a Catholic festival. The celebration in Rio is the most well-known Carnival in the world. Modern celebrations in Rio focus on the parade of samba schools the Sunday night before Ash Wednesday. These schools are neighborhood organizations that coordinate music, dancing, costumes, and floats around a particular theme that changes every year. The first school was organized in 1928, shortly after samba music became popular. Now there are more than fifty schools located around the city. Most of the participants come from the poorer sections of Rio society.

Planning and practicing for Carnival begins one year ahead of time and provides a focus for community life in poor areas. Each school designs a theme for the parade. They write a samba that reflects the theme in its words and music and design costumes and dances to portray the theme to spectators.

Below: **Carnival celebrations in Rio are very elaborate. Anywhere from 3,000 to 30,000 people may participate in each samba school. Some dance in beautiful costumes, others play in the percussion section, others ride the floats, and still others work behind the scenes making costumes or writing music.**

Judging Carnival

Beginning Sunday evening and lasting well into the next day, the schools parade through the Sambadrome, a stadium specifically designed for this purpose by Oscar Niemeyer. Schools are judged on their originality, choreography, costumes, floats, music, and organization. Each school has a rank in one of three leagues and competes for the top ranking or to move up in the leagues. Judges are local artists, writers, and musicians.

Participating in Carnival

Everyone takes part in Carnival. Those not in the parade line the streets or go to the Sambadrome to watch the parade. They dance and sing along with the schools. It is a test of endurance to try to dance all night as the parade files by. In addition to the parade, there are street parties during the official days of Carnival (Saturday night to noon on Ash Wednesday). On the last night, the party moves to Rio's nightclubs, where everyone celebrates all night. Carnival is virtually a national celebration, with the party in Rio being the biggest of them all!

Above: **A child dressed up for Carnival enjoys a clown's company.**

Chico Mendes: A Martyr to the Cause

In 1970, the Transamazonian Highway was built by the military government to open the forest to developers. Businessmen from southern Brazil sent workers to bulldoze the trees, burn them, and grow grass for cattle. When the cattle ranches started threatening the lands of the rubber-tappers, the latter organized *empates* (aym-PAH-tays), or peaceful stand-offs. Between 1976 and 1988, some forty-five empates prevented destruction of over 2,471,000 acres (1 million hectares) of forest. However, many protesting tappers and their families were murdered by hired thugs — ninety of these people died in 1988 alone.

Above: Latex collected from a rubber tree.

Left: A rubber-tapper hard at work smoking latex, while a child observes him.

Chico Mendes' Murder

Chico Mendes was the leader of the Xapuri Rural Workers' Union in Acre. Due to his important position in this organization and his active opposition to the destruction of the Amazon rain forest by owners of large cattle herds, Mendes was killed. Mendes' murder made international newspaper headlines and attracted world attention to the problems occurring in the rain forest. Partly as a result of this media attention, the Brazilian government moved quickly to establish and legalize special reserves of land called extractive reserves. These are areas of the rain forest set aside for traditional rubber-tappers, where they can continue to extract rubber and other resources. They cannot sell the land to outsiders, and they cannot destroy the forest. Ten such extractive reserves now exist, but their longevity depends on whether or not the rubber-tappers can make a living. Sadly, Mendes had more effect on the government in death than in life.

Above: **A woman reads a wall painting in remembrance of Chico Mendes.**

Below: **Chico Mendes.**

Economic Miracle: Miracle for Whom?

Industrial Growth

Brazil's "economic miracle" was the rapid and dramatic increase in production in an economy created by huge investment projects under the military dictatorship. Since the return to civilian rule in 1985, Brazil has had to rethink the "miracle" and how much it really cost the Brazilian people. The industries that grew provided jobs for those with the right skills. The managers and owners certainly made lots of money, but for the majority of Brazilians, the "miracle" was a disaster. According to the United Nations, Brazil has one of the largest differences in income in the world between the rich and poor. The "miracle" drove the poor into deeper poverty by focusing only on large-scale production. There were no incentives for smaller industries or protection of workers' rights. The inflation that has plagued the country since the debt crisis has made life a misery for those who are unemployed, underemployed, or employed in low-wage jobs.

CRIME IN BRAZIL

Massive and widespread poverty has contributed to high crime rates all over Brazil. In the cities, there are pickpockets, and theft is often accompanied by violence. In the countryside, the fight for survival is so desperate that people resort to murder to protect their land or to get access to it.

Below: A shantytown in Rio.

The Suffering Poor

The poorest families cannot afford to feed their children, so they abandon them to life on the streets in cities like São Paulo, Rio, and Salvador. Some of the oldest shantytowns have gained title to their land and are fighting for services like electricity and water, but the new ones formed by rural migrants chased off their land by large agricultural businesses live in the worst imaginable conditions.

One way the government has tried to deal with poverty is to open the Amazon to development. Development, however, has resulted in damage to the forest and impossible living conditions for many settlers. Settlers arrive by bus along nearly impassable roads, slave to open their land to farming by cutting and burning the forest, grow crops for a couple of years, then abandon the land when it is no longer productive. The result of these programs is that the poor are still poor, and the forest is disappearing. It is doubtful whether the "miracle" was truly miraculous except for those at the top of Brazilian society.

Above: **Some families living in shantytowns survive by scavenging in garbage dumps. No one is excused from this work, not even young children.**

Kayapo: Symbols of the Forest

Kayapo Indians

The Kayapo Indians are a group of about three thousand indigenous people living in Brazil's lush rain forest. Like many of Brazil's 250,000 indigenous people, they are now facing destruction of both their culture and their lives as a result of the economic development of the rain forest by individuals and big companies. The story of the Kayapo is one that is sadly repeated with many Indian cultures. The one difference is that the Kayapo have captured world attention because of the relationship between one Kayapo chief, Raoni, and the famous rock star, Sting.

Below: **Sting (seated second from right) and Raoni (seated first from left). Kayapo Indians live in small semi-permanent settlements scattered throughout the jungle. They traditionally depend on hunting, fishing, and gardening for food.**

The Buzz about Sting and Raoni

Sting met Raoni in Brazil in 1989. During this meeting, Sting learned about the plight of Raoni's people, who were being killed and pushed off their land by greedy gold miners and loggers. Sting called a press conference in May 1989 to tell the world what was happening to these people. Later the same year, Sting and his actress wife, Trudie Styler, founded the Rainforest Foundation, a charity dedicated to saving both the rain forest and its Indian inhabitants. The Rainforest Foundation still exists, and its main office is located in New York. In 1995, it extended its work to all rain forests and their dwellers.

In 1990, Sting took Raoni on a world tour to let him tell his own story, which put a lot of international public pressure on the Brazilian government to make changes in its Indian policy. In 1992, the Earth Summit was held in Brazil, and Raoni made a plea to the international community to help him save his people's land. Finally, in 1993, the government announced the creation of a special reserve in the forest where Raoni's people can live undisturbed by outsiders. However, despite international media attention, real solutions to forest preservation and protection of indigenous cultures are not easily available.

Below: **Kayapo warriors performing a war dance.**

The Problem Remains

Reserves exist for some Indian groups, but they are not policed. Miners and loggers trespass on Indian land and are still a direct threat to Indian people. Trespassing occurs because farmers, loggers, and miners working in the forest cannot access other land because it is controlled by large owners who do not want to share.

Move That Body!

Since earliest colonial times, Brazil has been a place where different musical traditions meet and blend to create new and wonderful forms. Deriving from both Portuguese and African cultural heritage, Brazilian musical forms have combined traditional and modern instruments in unique ways. Samba and bossa nova have made Brazilian music world famous.

Above: **Carmen Miranda's rise to fame began in Brazil in 1930 when she signed a recording contract with RCA Victor.**

Samba

In 1917, the first official samba song, "On the Phone," was copyrighted in Rio de Janeiro. The first composers of samba music were transplanted Bahians of African ancestry. The first samba school was founded in 1928. Samba became popular outside Brazil largely as a result of the popularity of Carmen Miranda. Born in Portugal but raised in Brazil, she was cast in the Broadway musical *Streets of Paris* in 1939. She became known in North America as the Brazilian Bombshell and the Ambassadress of the samba.

Left: **Gilberto Gil plays a guitar. Gil and Caetano Veloso were a huge success in Brazil and Europe.**

Bossa Nova

One of the more recent offshoots of samba is bossa nova, which is a slightly jazzier samba with complicated guitar playing and subdued vocal accompaniment. It was the product of the combined talents of João Gilberto and Antônio Carlos "Tom" Jobim. In the late 1950s and early 1960s, people were humming bossa nova classics such as "The Girl from Ipanema," "One Note Samba," "Quiet Nights of Quiet Stars," and "Foolishness."

During the military dictatorship, two songwriters, Caetano Veloso and Gilberto Gil, became famous for their sound, known as Tropicalism. Because they could not have their music broadcast, they took self-exile in London, England, from 1969 to 1972. Tropicalism used electric guitars and back-up singers and was much louder and wilder than previous forms of bossa nova.

Pelé: King of Soccer

A Talent Discovered

Along with Carnival and samba, Pelé, the "King of Soccer," has made Brazil famous worldwide. In 1940, Pelé was born Édson Arantes do Nascimento in Minas Gerais to a poor family. The family moved to São Paulo when he was young, and Édson learned soccer by watching his father and playing in the street with other children. Street soccer is called *peladas* (pay-LAH-dahs). The name "Pelé" comes from this word. When he was fifteen years old, Pelé was asked to join one of São Paulo's professional teams, the Santos Football Club. He played his first professional game at the age of sixteen. He was so good that, the following year, he was chosen to play with Brazil's national team in the upcoming World Cup. The World Cup is played every four years by teams that qualify in their regions all over the world. Brazil qualified in 1958 and, with the help of Pelé's six goals, won the cup for the first time.

Above and *left:* **What captured everyone's imagination about Pelé, aside from his humble beginnings, was his amazing footwork. He is compared to a dancer with the soccer ball. Even today, legions of fans remember him.**

An Amazing Career

Pelé made the national team again in 1962 and, even though he was injured, helped the team win its second consecutive World Cup. Brazil qualified again in 1966, but many members of the team were injured, and Brazil did not play in the finals. Pelé played his last World Cup in 1970 in Mexico City at the age of thirty. Many soccer fans consider the finals of this World Cup to be the most exciting ever. The Brazilian team played wonderfully and went on to take home its third World Cup. Pelé was named Most Valuable Player of the tournament. Pelé continued to play in Brazil until 1974 when he retired from the Santos Club.

Left: Pelé in action in the 1958 World Cup final. In 1975, Pelé decided to return to soccer. He joined the New York Cosmos of the North American Soccer League and played with them for two years. Although the League does not exist anymore, Pelé is credited with popularizing the sport in the United States.

São Paulo

History

São Paulo was founded by two Jesuit priests in 1554 when they established a mission for Indians on a plateau. For the next three hundred years, São Paulo was a base for the *bandeirantes* (bahn-day-RAHN-tays), mixed Portuguese-Indian explorers who traveled to the interior looking for Indians and gold. The population of São Paulo grew to 65,000 by the 1890s.

When plantation owners started coffee production in the 1860s, São Paulo started to boom. The plantation owners faced constant labor shortages, so in 1870, they started to encourage immigration from abroad. Over the next fifty years, five million immigrants arrived in the state, with about half settling in the city. Around the turn of the century, the coffee estate owners decided to invest in other types of businesses. They chose manufacturing, and São Paulo has never looked back.

Below: São Paulo's huge, gleaming corporate offices and luxury high-rises. However, one must not forget the *favelas* (fah-VAY-lahs). These are areas around the downtown core, where people live in tin and wooden shacks. Such neighborhoods usually lack street lights, water, and sewage service.

São Paulo Today

Residents of the city of São Paulo, *Paulistanos* (pow-leesh-TAHN-ohs), hustle and bustle and produce the largest share of Brazil's industrial economy. The city teems with activity. The artistic and musical communities thrive, but all is not perfect for residents of this metropolis.

For one, most industrial production has been unregulated, meaning there are no pollution controls. The area between São Paulo and Santos (on the coast) is called Cubatão, which is known to be the most dangerous environment in the world because of the concentration of toxic waste from chemical plants and other industries. The government is trying to clean up the area, but it is still an environmental nightmare.

On a more positive note, descendants of immigrants continue to add a touch of Europe or Asia to this South American giant. One area of interest to visitors and residents alike is the Liberdade, a little slice of Japan in the heart of São Paulo. This community was founded with the arrival of the first Japanese immigrants in 1908. Today, it still caters to the needs of Japanese-Brazilians and attracts visitors to its restaurants and gift shops.

Above: **People shop and visit at an open-air market in São Paulo.**

Slavery

Slavery built and propelled Brazil throughout its early history. Before the African slave trade developed in the seventeenth century, trade in Indian slaves from Brazil's interior flourished. The slave hunters, known as bandeirantes or *paulistas* (pow-LEESH-tahs), because their operations were based in São Paulo, ranged far inland in search of Indians to transport to the sugar fields of the northeast. The slave traders were often of mixed European and Indian descent. They were the first to discover gold in the rivers of Minas Gerais, sparking the first gold rush in 1690.

African slaves first arrived in Portuguese settlements in 1532; they did so for the next 320 years. About one hundred thousand Africans arrived in Brazil in the sixteenth century; two million in the seventeenth century; two million in the eighteenth century; and about 1.5 million in the first half of the nineteenth century, before slave trade was finally outlawed in 1852.

Below: **An illustration that shows slaves buying tobacco.**

All industries developed in Brazil from the late sixteenth century until the nineteenth century were founded on slave labor. Brazilians were thus reluctant to join the movement to end slavery in the nineteenth century. Britain ended slavery in the Caribbean in the 1830s and started pressuring other countries to do the same. Since slave labor was cheaper, British colonies could not compete in price with countries still permitting slavery. Brazil held out until the British threatened war in the 1850s. At this point, Brazil ended the trade in slaves but did not free the slaves that were already in the country. Abolition came in 1888, when slave revolts had become so frequent that it was no longer economical or safe to continue the practice.

The history of slavery of Indians and Africans continues to be significant for modern Brazil. Culturally, Brazil is a blend of European, Indian, and African traditions. Language, art, music, and religion are all heavily influenced by African cultures from West Africa, the origin of the majority of slaves. In the twentieth century, racial blending through mixed marriages continues. However, the stigma of slavery remains. In general terms, black and Indian Brazilians are still poorest and often experience discrimination.

Above: Brazilians are quite mixed racially. Many, if not most, Brazilians whose families have been there since colonial times can trace some of their ancestry to Indian or African origins. Part of the reason for this racial mix is also that many original Portuguese settlers married Indian and African women.

The Written Word

Illiteracy remains a big problem in Brazil. Despite this, Brazilian writers have made their mark on readers at home and abroad. After the nineteenth century, Brazilian writers tried to imitate the styles of continental Europe, thinking Europeans defined art and literature for the world. In February 1922, an event called Modern Art Week marked a definite shift away from this attitude toward creating distinctly Brazilian art and writing.

Joaquim Maria Machado de Assis

Joaquim Maria Machado de Assis (1839–1908) was an amazing writer who broke with the European tradition even before it became fashionable in the 1920s. He founded the Brazilian Academy of Letters and was its first president. His novels and short stories have all been translated into English. Some titles include *Esau and Jacob* (1904) and *Epitaph of a Small Winner* (1880).

Above: Translated into English as *Gabriela, Clove and Cinnamon*, this book by Jorge Amado has also become well-known in the English-speaking world.

Left: English literary critics have declared Machado de Assis the greatest author ever produced in Latin America — that is quite a compliment given the rich literary tradition of the continent.

Jorge Amado

Born in 1912, Jorge Amado may be the writer best known outside Brazil. He is from the northeast and focuses most of his novels on Salvador, where he lives. Most of his books tell stories about the blacks of Salvador and often have very strong female characters. Amado was involved in social protest movements in the 1930s and 1940s, and this concern is reflected in his stories. His books have been widely translated and one, *Dona Flor and Her Two Husbands*, was made into a film that broke box office records in Brazil in 1980. Other well-known titles are *Tent of Miracles* (1971), *Gabriela, Clove and Cinnamon* (1962), *Jubiabá* (1984), and *The War of the Saints* (1993).

Graciliano Ramos

Graciliano Ramos (1892–1953) was one of the many writers to be influenced by the ideas of Modern Art Week. He was from the backlands of the northeast, and all of his novels portray life in these poor and difficult conditions. For example, *Barren Lives* (1930) is about a family dealing with drought and hardship in the sertão. His other books deal with human psychology and the role of women in Brazilian society.

RELATIONS WITH NORTH AMERICA

No country can be understood in isolation. All national history and culture is shaped partly in response to foreign influences. How Brazilian culture has been shaped by Portuguese and African influences has already been discussed. This section will take a closer look at Brazil's historical relationship with the United States, as well as how this relationship has changed over time. Some Brazilians have immigrated to the United States and Canada. They are known as *Brazucos* (brah-ZOO-cohs) and have brought their customs, including food and celebrations, with them. Some Americans also live in Brazil. This section will also consider how Brazilian culture has influenced American culture, especially in terms of music and dance, and what Brazilian culture has to offer the rest of the world.

Opposite: **The Christ the Redeemer statue in Rio.**

Below: **Brazilian children with sparkling and engaging smiles.**

History of Brazil–U.S. Relations

Relations between these two giants have been fairly friendly in the past. The United States was the first country to recognize Brazil's independence in 1822, and Emperor Pedro II visited the United States during the centenary of American independence in 1876. Since then, U.S. presidents Theodore and Franklin Delano Roosevelt, Truman, Eisenhower, Reagan, Carter, and Clinton all have visited Brazil. Brazilian President José Sarney visited the United States in 1986.

In 1913, former U.S. president Theodore Roosevelt was part of an exploratory mission to the Amazon. With Brazilian explorer Candido Rondon, Roosevelt led an expedition to prove the existence of a tributary of the Amazon River. He was fifty-five years old at the time but survived the harrowing journey into the rain forest. They found the mythical river, and in his honor, the name of the river was changed from "River of Doubt" to "Roosevelt River." In the early part of the twentieth century, the Amazon attracted other Americans interested in developing its vast resources. Henry Ford created rubber plantations in 1927 at sites called Fordlândia and Belterra near the Amazon River. Due to poor disease control, Ford's plantations failed.

Under President Getúlio Vargas, Brazil declared its support for the Allies in 1942 when the United States entered World War II. That year, Brazilian ships were sunk by Axis forces; this prompted Vargas to send 25,000 troops to Europe. They were called the Brazilian Expeditionary Force and participated in the Italian campaign in Europe from 1944 to 1945. Brazil was the only country in Latin America to send troops to fight with the Allies, thus solidifying growing ties of friendship between the United States and Brazil.

From the end of World War II to the 1970s, Brazil and the United States maintained positive relations. The United States was Brazil's main trading partner and established programs to help Brazil improve its economy. In the 1950s and 1960s, the Agency for International Development (AID) and Food for Peace loaned Brazil a total of $2.4 billion dollars. There were programs to train Brazilians in modern technology as well as donations and loans of goods and information. The Peace Corps was also active in Brazil until 1980. As Brazil's economy became stronger throughout the late 1960s and 1970s, these programs were phased out. The relationship between these two great nations also became more complicated as Brazil emerged as a significant world economic power.

Above: **Memorabilia of Brazilian soldiers who died in battle during World War II.**

Left: **Brazilian soldiers doing their part during World War II.**

Current Brazil–U.S. Relations

In the last twenty-five years, Brazil–U.S. relations have changed significantly. Once, Brazil was treated like any other third-world nation, but now it demands and deserves a different kind of relationship with the powerful North American industrial nations. For example, Brazil argued in the 1970s that, as a large industrial economy, it had the right to use nuclear energy and produce nuclear weapons. The United States refused to send the necessary technology, so, in 1977, Brazil arranged a deal with West Germany to acquire plutonium and nuclear power technology. Brazil refused to sign away its right to produce nuclear weapons or to allow international inspectors into Brazil. It opened the first nuclear power station in 1985 but closed it for safety reasons in 1987. Today, however, Brazil has signed an international treaty to stop producing nuclear weapons.

Brazil has tried to reduce its dependency on the United States by trading with other countries and making its own arms and weapons. Due to massive borrowing in the 1960s and 1970s, Brazil owed a huge sum of money to U.S. banks and international

Above: **The Brazilian army. Today, it is less dependent on foreign-manufactured arms and U.S. funds.**

lending agencies. This debt caused further problems. Brazil argued that the United States put unfair import taxes on Brazilian exports to the United States so they could not compete with U.S. products. Brazil also argued that if the country was not allowed to sell its goods, then it could not earn enough to pay its debts.

On its part, the United States charged Brazil with unfair trade practices. Brazil formerly did not protect international patents. In the 1980s, a Brazilian company could take a computer apart and learn how to manufacture it without paying for the knowledge. In the 1990s, however, Brazil has signed a patents treaty with the United States that includes both computers and software.

In the early 1990s, a suggested solution to the debt problem was a debt-for-nature swap. This aimed to trade debt or money owed by poorer countries for the protection of the environment, by setting aside land and resources as parks and reserves. Brazil participated in this program but disagreed with the idea of foreign control over its natural resources. Due to economic reform and increased stability, foreign debt is no longer as important an issue in Brazil. The two countries, meanwhile, have had successful agreements for working together on scientific research.

Below: **Despite Brazil's attempt to assert its identity, American culture still has a strong influence in Brazil.**

Brazilian Immigration to North America

Small numbers of Brazilians have lived in major U.S. cities, such as New York and Washington D.C., for a long time. Most of them work for Brazilian companies or government diplomatic offices. In the mid-1980s, however, Brazilians began arriving in the United States in large numbers to work as illegal immigrants.

Since about 1985, the economy in Brazil has been very unstable. The middle class were most affected by economic problems as the standard of living plunged. These are the people most likely to immigrate to the United States and Canada. They are usually educated and hope to find work that will allow them to send some money home to their families to help them combat inflation and enjoy some economic stability.

Estimates range from 300,000 to 600,000 Brazilians currently living in the United States, most of them illegally. The main destinations for Brazilians, or Brazucos as they are known in the United States, include New York, San Francisco, Los Angeles, Washington D.C., and Boston, and Toronto in Canada.

Below: **Brazucos walking dogs. Although most Brazucos have high school and even college or university training, they end up working in low-paying, unskilled jobs in the United States and Canada, usually because they do not speak good English. As illegal workers, they cannot apply for jobs where they will have to show a green card. People who employ illegals pay them much less than the minimum wage and offer no job security or benefits.**

Left: **Brazilians in the United States enjoy themselves on Brazilian Independence Day.**

Slices of Brazil

Some Brazucos plan to stay only a few years. They want to save enough money to start a business or buy property back in Brazil. Others hope to return home one day, but have no fixed goals. Still others have no intention of going back to Brazil and hope to become legal residents of the United States or Canada. This last group will eventually blend into the mosaic of North America like so many immigrant groups before them. As long-term residents, they are already establishing services and activities for themselves and changing their neighborhoods into little slices of Brazil.

One good example of this phenomenon is "Little Brazil" in Manhattan, a short stretch of 46th Street between Fifth Avenue and Avenue of the Americas. There have been Brazilian businesses and restaurants here since the 1960s, but since the large influx of Brazucos started in the 1980s, this area has become a vibrant focus of the New York Brazilian population. Every September, there is a street party here to celebrate Brazilian Independence Day. The last celebration attracted thousands of people and rivals the more formal celebrations at the Brazilian consulate for attracting Brazucos.

Above: **Tourists admire the beauty of Iguaçu Falls.**

Americans in Brazil

Many Americans and Canadians currently work in Brazil. Some of them relocate at least temporarily. Many North Americans also travel to Brazil as tourists. The prime attractions are Carnival in Rio and the endless miles of beautiful beaches. Brazilian tourism has suffered recently because of the bad economy and perceptions of high crime rates in its major cities. At the same time, more and more North Americans are interested in visiting exotic countries; South America is a favorite destination because it is nearby.

The Amazon attracts many scientists interested in both animal and plant life and in the indigenous people. Anthropologists from the United States and Canada have been working for a long time to understand the cultures and languages of the many groups living there. The United States and Brazil have exchange programs such as the Fulbright Scholarship, which allows professors from each country to swap places for a year and participate in university research in the other country.

There was a time when significant numbers of Americans moved to Brazil to live. Following the Civil War in the United States in 1865, a group of southerners led by an Alabama state senator, Colonel William Hutchinson Norris, arrived in São Paulo. Hutchinson purchased a farm about 80 miles (129 km) northwest of São Paulo, where the first group of settlers lived and worked. They grew cotton and watermelons. Between 1867 and 1871, approximately three thousand American southerners arrived every year to live in Brazil. Many of them became homesick and returned to the United States, but at the turn of the century, there was still a small group living at Hutchinson's settlement, which they named Americana. The descendants of these people call themselves Confederados, after the Confederate States, and still celebrate their American origins. Every April, the Confederados have a reunion just outside Americana. They dress up in Civil War costumes and eat hot dogs and candied apples. The women wear large hoop skirts and the men wear Confederate Army uniforms. They display the Confederate flag and honor the four hundred or so Americans buried in a cemetery near Americana. Americana has also become a center for the textile industry in Brazil.

Below: **Americans enjoy themselves in the Amazon.**

Left: Stan Getz in his element. One of America's greatest saxophone players, he collaborated with Brazilian guitarist João Gilberto and his wife Astrud in 1963 to make the most popular bossa nova album of the time: *Getz/Gilberto*. The album won four Grammy Awards and was on the pop charts for ninety-six weeks! It is still produced today because of its enduring popularity.

Musical Influences

The main area of cultural exchange between North America and Brazil is music. Brazilian samba in the form of bossa nova was incredibly popular in North America in the 1960s. Brazilian youths have also become fans of North American and European rock musicians. This influence is apparent in the 1980s trend of Rock Brasileiro (Brazilian Rock). Such music incorporates some elements of North American rock music, with lyrics being far more direct than traditional, Brazilian romantic ballads.

Dance the Night Away

Latin American dance forms have become very popular in Europe and North America in the last fifteen years. The samba has migrated along with Brazucos to nightclubs in U.S. and Canadian cities. It is not only Brazucos who dance the samba in the north; the Cheremoya Samba School in Hollywood is all-American, from its creators, Lee Cobim and Linda Yudin, to its participants.

Fashion and the Future

While few North American dance traditions can compete with vibrant Brazilian forms, North American youth fashion is still the trend-setter for South Americans. A university or high school student in Brazil is not likely to look much different from his or her counterpart in North America. Since Brazilian immigration to North America is still fairly recent, Brazilian food has not become popular yet. As these new North Americans settle in, however, enjoying feijoada at Brazilian restaurants in Canada and the United States may be common in the near future.

Left: **The Lambada was a Brazilian dance craze that spread around the world in the early 1990s.**

	A	B	C	D

1

VENEZUELA

GUYANA

COLOMBIA

SURINAME

FRENCH GUIANA

G U I A N A   H I G H L A N D S

RORAIMA

AMAPÁ

Equ...

2

A m a z o n

MARAJÓ ISLAND

●**Belém**

◆**Manaus**

●**Fordlândia**

AMAZONAS

PARÁ

MARANHÃO

CEARÁ

RIO GRANDE NORTE

PARAÍBA

PIAUÍ

Olinda
Reci

PERNAMBUCO

ACRE

RONDÔNIA

R o o s e v e l t

B R A Z I L I A N   H I G H L A N D S

TOCANTINS

ALAGOAS

SERGIPE

3

PERU

MATO GROSSO

S ã o   F r a n c i s c o

BAHIA

◆**Salvador**

All Saints Bay (Baía de Todos os Sa...

**Federal District
(Distrito Federal)**

A N D E S   M O U N T A I N S

BOLIVIA

Pantanal

■**BRASÍLIA**

GOIÁS

MINAS GERAIS

▲**Porto Seguro**

▲Mt. Pascoal

●

PACIFIC
OCEAN

MATO GROSSO
DO SUL

P a r a n á

SÃO PAULO

Belo Horizonte
◆

ESPÍRITO
SANTO

4

PARAGUAY

Americana
●

Ouro Preto
●

**Rio de
Janeiro**

RIO DE JANEIRO

*Iguaçu
Falls*

PARANÁ

**São
Paulo**

Cubatão◆

◆

Santos

▲ Sugar Loaf Mountain

A T L A N T I C   O C E A N

Tropic of Cap...

CHILE

A N D E S   M O U N T A I N S

SANTA CATARINA

●**Florianópolis**

ARGENTINA

RIO GRANDE
DO SUL

5

URUGUAY

Rio Plata

BRAZIL

Legend:
— State Boundary
- - - Tropic of Capricorn
■ National Capital
● City
~ River
◆ State Capitals

N

Above: Soaking up sun at a beach along Brazil's beautiful coastline.

Acre A3
Alagoas D3
All Saints Bay D3
Amapá C2
Amazon River A2-C2
Amazonas A2
Americana C4
Andes Mountains A3–A5
Argentina B5
Atlantic Ocean D4-D5

Bahia D3
Belém C2
Belo Horizonte C4
Bolivia A3–A4
Brasília C4
Brazilian Highlands B3

Ceará D2
Chile A4-A5
Colombia A1
Cubatão C4

Distrito Federal C4

Espírito Santo D4

Florianópolis C5

Fordlândia B2
French Guiana C1

Goiás C4
Guiana Highlands B2
Guyana B1

Iguaçu Falls B4

Manaus B2
Marajó Island C2
Maranhão C2
Mato Grosso B3
Mato Grosso do Sul
   B4–C4
Minas Gerais C4
Mount Pascoal D4

Olinda D3
Ouro Preto D4

Pacific Ocean A4
Pantanal B4
Pará C2
Paraguay B4
Paraíba D3
Paraná C4
Paraná River C4

Pernambuco D3
Peru A3
Piauí C3
Porto Seguro D4

Rio de Janeiro (city) C4
Rio de Janeiro (state) D4
Rio Grande do Norte D2
Rio Grande do Sul
   B5–C5
Rio Plata B5
Rondônia B3
Roosevelt River B3
Roraima B2
Recife D3

Salvador D3
Santa Catarina C5
Santos C4
São Francisco River D3
São Paulo (city) C4
São Paulo (state) C4
Sergipe D3
Sugar Loaf Mountain D4
Suriname B2

Tocantins C3

Uruguay B5

Venezuela A1

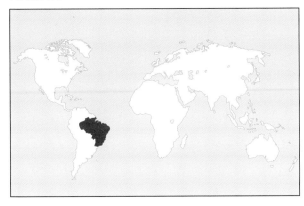

A B C D

N

1

2

Equ

3

4

Tropic of Cap

5

BRAZIL

How Is Your Geography?

Learning to identify the main geographical areas and points of a country can be challenging. Although it may seem difficult at first to memorize the location and spelling of major cities or the names of mountain ranges, rivers, deserts, lakes, and other prominent physical features, the end result of this effort can be very rewarding. Places you previously did not know existed will suddenly come to life when referred to in world news, whether in newspapers, television reports, or other books and reference sources. This knowledge will make you feel a bit closer to the rest of the world, with its fascinating variety of cultures and physical geographies.

Used in a classroom setting, the instructor can make duplicates of this map using a copy machine (PLEASE DO NOT WRITE IN THIS BOOK!). Students can then fill in any requested information on their individual map copies. Used one-on-one, the student can also make copies of the map on a copy machine and use them as a study tool. The student can practice identifying place names and geographical features on his or her own.

Below: **Bringing in the catch from Lake Conceicao in Florianópolis.**

Brazil at a Glance

Official Name República Federativa do Brasil, Federative Republic of Brazil

Capital Brasília

Official Language Portuguese is spoken by all but a tiny minority of Indian peoples.

Population 160 million

Ethnic Groups 55 percent European origin; 38.5 percent mulattoes; 5 percent African origin; 1.5 percent Indian

Land Area 3,286,487 square miles (8,512,001 square kilometers)

States Acre, Alagoas, Amapá, Amazonas, Bahia, Brasília (located in the Federal District), Ceará, Espírito Santo, Goiás, Maranhão, Mato Grosso, Mato Grosso do Sul, Minas Gerais, Pará, Paraíba, Paraná, Pernambuco, Piauí, Rio de Janeiro, Río Grande do Norte, Rio Grande do Sul, Rondônia, Roraima, Santa Catarina, São Paulo, Sergipe, Tocantins

Highest point Pico de Neblina at 9,888 feet (3,014 meters) above sea level

Major River Amazon River

Important Festivals Iemanjá Festival, Lord Jesus of Seafarers; Bonfim Festival; Carnival; Easter; Labor Day; June Festivals; Independence Celebrations; Our Lady Aparecida; All Soul's Day; Proclamation of the Republic; Christmas

National Anthem *Ouviram do Ipiranga as margens plácidas*, "From Peaceful Ipiranga's Banks Rang Out a Cry"

Flag A green field with a large yellow diamond in the middle. In the center of the diamond is a blue globe with a white banner around it. Below the banner are the constellations of the southern skies and above is a single star. The banner reads "Ordem e Progresso," meaning "Order and Progress." Green stands for forests, while yellow represents gold.

Currency Brazilian Real (1.15 real = U.S. $1 as of 1998)

Opposite: **A blaze of color at the Carnival celebrations in Rio.**

Glossary

Brazilian Vocabulary

acarajé (ah-cahr-AH-zhay): Bahian hamburger made from a type of bean mashed up with ground shrimp and onion, then deep fried and served with chilies.

axé (AH-shay): divine energy. Candomblé followers believe that humans and nature have this energy.

bacalhau (bah-kahl-YOW): Portuguese dried codfish.

bandeirantes (bahn-day-RAHN-tays): explorers of mixed Portuguese and Indian descent who went into the interior regions of Brazil.

Brazucos (brah-ZOO-cohs): Brazilians living in the United States.

cachaça (kah-CHAH-sah): alcohol made from sugarcane juice.

Cafusos (cah-FOO-sohs): children of African and Indian parentage.

caipirinha (kye-peer-EEN-yah): Brazilian national drink made with sugarcane alcohol, lime, and sugar.

candomblé (cahn-DOM-blay): a mystical religion practiced by Brazilians in the northeast.

capoeira (kah-poh-EYR-ah): a type of musical kickboxing.

carrancas (kahr-RAN-kahs): carvings of monsters designed to fit the front of a boat and believed to frighten away evil spirits in the water.

cocada (ko-KAH-dah): coconut candy boiled in sugar water and flavored with lemon or sugar.

cordel (COR-dayl): stories about local heroes, sold in the northeast.

dendê (dayn-day): unrefined palm oil.

empates (aym-PAH-tays): peaceful stand-offs between rubber-tappers and developers.

favelas (fah-VAY-lahs): slums around major cities.

feijoada (fay-zhoh-AH-dah): Brazilian national dish made with black beans and meat.

gaiolas (gay-OHL-ahs): Literally meaning "birdcages," these boats carry people and cargo in cramped decks.

Mamelucos (mah-may-LOO-kohs): children of European and Indian parentage.

marajoara (mah-rah-joh-AHR-ah): a special type of pottery from the island of Marajó.

Mulatos (moo-LAH-tohs): children of African and European parentage.

orixás (oh-REE-shahs): spirits of the candomblé religion.

Paulistanos (pow-leesh-TAHN-ohs): people living in the city of São Paulo.

salgadinhos (sahl-gah-DEEN-yohs): small pastries filled with cheese, ham, shrimp, chicken, or beef.

sertão (sayr-TAO): highland area inland from the Atlantic coast, subject to periodic droughts.

telenovela (tay-lay-noh-VAY-lah): evening soap opera shown on television.

umbanda (oom-BAN-dah): religious cult worshiping Iemanjá, Queen of the Seas.

English Vocabulary

avidly: enthusiastically and energetically.

centenary: a span of 100 years.

consecutive: one after another without any break or lapse in between.

dependency: reliance on.

diverse: of many different types and varieties.

drought: a long period of dry weather.

elusive: very difficult to locate.

encroaching: moving into somebody else's territory without permission.

extensive: spread over a wide area or covering many details.

foreign debt: what is owed to other nations.

harrowing: acutely distressing.

icons: physical representations of certain ideas and concepts.

illiterates: people who are unable to read or write.

indigenous: native to a particular place.

isolated: not in contact, either physically or emotionally, with other people.

layoffs: loss of jobs during times of economic difficulty.

malaria: a disease in which the individual suffers from a fever, sweating, and chills. Malaria is spread by the *Anopheles* mosquito.

malnutrition: a physical condition that results when an individual does not receive required or sufficient nutrition over a prolonged period of time.

martyr: an individual who dies or undergoes tremendous suffering for certain beliefs or causes that are usually religious or political in nature.

meager: extremely little.

millenia: spans of 1,000 years.

mortality: death rates.

ornate: very detailed and intricate.

pamphlets: small, thin publications that provide information concerning a particular topic.

pastries: food baked from dough. Such foods are usually small, sweet, and may be eaten for breakfast or a snack.

plunge: to dip downward suddenly.

possessed: to be under the control of an external force such that an individual no longer has voluntary control over his or her own actions or thoughts.

prehensile: particularly well-suited for holding or hanging onto something.

recognition: acknowledgment of an individual's efforts and contributions to a particular area.

regent: someone who acts as ruler in the absence of the true one, or if the true ruler is still too young.

renowned: very well-known and widely acknowledged.

rubber-tappers: people who tap the latex, or milky juice, of rubber trees by cutting fine grooves into the tree. The latex hardens as it dries.

sherbets: desserts made of ice and fruit, similar to ice-cream.

spectacular: amazing, stupendous, and extremely impressive.

stigma: negative association.

tactician: an individual who is very skilled at planning tactics and strategies.

theme: predominant concept or idea.

thrive: to grow or develop very well.

traditions: established and customary methods of action or thought.

More Books to Read

An Adventure in the Amazon. The Costeau Society (Simon & Schuster)

Brazil. Country Fact Files series. Marion Morrison (Simon & Schuster)

Brazil. Cultures of the World series. Christopher Richard (Marshall Cavendish)

Brazil. Festivals of the World series. Susan McKay (Gareth Stevens Publishing)

Brazil. Places and Peoples of the World series. Evelyn Bender (Chelsea House Publishers)

Brazil. World in View series. Moyra Ashford (Steck-Vaughn Company)

The Brazilian Rainforest. Alexandra Siy (Dillon Press)

Christmas in Brazil. Rebecca Lauer (World Book, Inc.)

How Night Came from the Sea: A Story from Brazil. Mary-Joan Gerson
    (Little, Brown & Co.)

Latin American and Carribean Crafts. Judith Corwin (Franklin Watts)

Rainforest. Sticky Fingers series. Ting Morris and Neil Morris (Franklin Watts)

Rio de Janeiro. Cities of the World series. Deborah Kent (Children's Press)

Tropical Rainforests. Jean Hamilton (Silver Burdett Press)

Videos

Amazon: Snowstorm in the Jungle and Rigging for the Amazon. (Turner Home
    Entertainment)

Brazil Northeast Experience. (International Video Network)

Yanomami — Keepers of the Flame. (California State Polytechnic University)

Web Sites

darkwing.uoregon.edu/~sergiok/brasil.html

www.lonelyplanet.com/dest/sam/bra.htm

www.brazilnature.com/

pasture.ecn.purdue.edu/~agenhtml/agenmc/brazil/brazil.html

Due to the dynamic nature of the Internet, some web sites stay current longer than others. To find additional web sites, use a reliable search engine with one or more of the following keywords to help you locate information on Brazil. Keywords: *Amazon, Brazil, Pelé, Rio de Janeiro, samba, soccer.*

Index

acarajé 51
agreste 7
agriculture 18
Alagoas 7
Aleijadinho 30
Amado, Jorge 43, 73
Amazon rain forest 8, 43, 44, 45, 76
Amazon River 6, 8, 9, 33, 43, 46, 47, 76, 82
Amazonas 8
Americana 83
animals 8, 9, 44, 80, 82
architecture 12, 32
art 5, 30, 31, 32, 33, 48, 49, 50, 71, 72
Ash Wednesday 56, 57
Atlantic Ocean 6, 14, 18, 46
auto racing 37
axé 54

bacalhau 40
Bahia 6, 7, 26, 29, 43, 50, 51, 54, 55
Baianas 51
bandeirantes 68, 70
Baroque 32
beaches 5, 82
Belo Horizonte 7
Bonfim Festival 55
bossa nova 63, 64, 65, 84
Brasília 5, 6, 9, 12, 16, 17, 27, 30, 32
Brazucos 75, 80, 81, 84
Bueno, Maria 37

Cabral, Pedro Álvares 14
cachaça 40
Cafusos 20
caipirinha 40
Canada 75, 80, 81, 82, 84, 85
candomblé 26, 27, 43, 49, 54, 55
capoeira 37

Cardoso, Fernando Henrique 13, 17
carioca 28
Carnival 38, 43, 56, 57, 82
carrancas 27
Catholics 26
Chamber of Deputies 16, 17
Cheremoya Samba School 84
children 20, 21, 22, 23, 24, 25, 61
Christmas 39
Círio de Nazaré 39
class 21, 22
coffee 7, 11, 18, 19, 41
comic books 29
Confederados 83
conversation 35
cordel 29
Costa, Lúcio 32
cotton 18, 33
Cravo, Mário 30
crime 60, 82
"Cry of Ipiranga" 38
Cubatão 69
cult members 27
custards 41

da Mota e Silva, Djanira 33
dance 75, 84, 85
da Silva, José Antônio 48
da Silva Xavier, José Joaquim 14
de Assis, Joaquim Maria Machado 72
de Jesús, Isabel 49
de Noronha, Fernando 7
dendê 51
desserts 41, 51
Dias, Henrique 14
Dom João 11

economy 21, 23, 24, 60, 61, 77, 78, 80, 82

education 22, 23, 24
empates 58
ethnicity 20
evening meal 41
exchange programs 82
exports 19, 79

family life 21, 24, 25, 61
farming 19
favelas 68
federal republic 16
feijoada 40, 85
Fittipaldi, Emerson 37
flag 5
food 23, 40, 41, 51, 85
Ford, Henry 76
foreign debt 13, 78, 79
forest (*see* rain forest)
forest preservation 45, 63

gaiolas 47
gender roles 25
geography 6-9
Germany 19
Getz, Stan 84
Gil, Gilberto 65
Gilberto, João 65, 84
godparenthood 24
Goiás 9
gold 10, 13, 19, 52, 53
Goulart, João 12
government 16, 17, 52, 59, 61

handicrafts 33
health care 23
history 10-15
hydroelectric power 18, 19

Iguaçu Falls 8, 82
illiteracy 17, 29, 72
imports 19, 79
Inconfidência Mineira 14
independence 12, 38, 76, 81

infant mortality 23
informal adoption 24
Itamaraty Palace 32

Japanese-Brazilians 69
Jesuit priests 68
Jobim, Antônio 65

Kayapo 18, 43, 62, 63
Kubitschek, Juscelino 12

Lacerda, Maria 49
lambada 85
language 28, 29, 71, 82
leisure 34, 35
Liberdade 69
"Little Brazil" 81

malagueta 51
Mamelucos 20
Manaus 7, 8, 31
manioc 40
marajoara 33
Maranhão 7
marriage 25, 71
Mato Grosso 9
Mato Grosso do Sul 9
Mendes, Chico 15, 58, 59
mercury poisoning 53
middle class 21, 22, 24, 80
Minas Gerais 7, 10, 13, 14, 31,
    32, 33, 66, 70
Miranda, Carmen 64
missionaries 32
Modern Art Week 48, 72, 73
moqueca 51
Mount Pascoal 14
mulattoes 20, 21, 50
music 5, 31, 37, 43, 50, 56, 57,
    64, 65, 71, 75, 84, 85
mysticism 27

natural resources 5, 6, 18,
    19, 79
New Year's Day 39
Niemeyer, Oscar 32, 57

northeast 6, 7, 22, 23, 29, 73
nuclear energy 78

Olympics 37
orixás 54
Ouro Preto 31, 32

Pantanal 9
Pará 8
Paraíba 6, 7
Paraná 6, 8
Paulistanos 69
Pedro I 11, 38
Pedro II 11, 15, 76
peladas 66
Pelé 36, 43, 66, 67
Pernambuco 7
Piauí 7
Piquet, Nelson 37
playwrights 31
Porto Seguro 14
possession 54, 55
pottery 33
poverty 21, 60
Prazeres, Heitor dos 48, 49
primary education 22
"primitive" art 48
Princess Isabel 11, 15
puddings 41

rain forests 5, 7, 8, 9, 18, 44,
    45, 63
Rainforest Foundation 63
rainstick 33
Ramos, Graciliano 73
religion 26, 39, 54, 71
Rio de Janeiro 5, 7, 13, 17, 21,
    28, 29, 34, 36, 37, 43, 56, 57,
    60, 61, 64, 75, 82
Rio Grande do Norte 7
Rio Grande do Sul 8
Rock Brasileiro 84
Rondon, Candido 76
Rondônia 8
Roosevelt River 76
Roosevelt, Theodore 76

Roraima 8
rubber-tappers 58, 59
Salvador 6, 37, 39, 55, 61, 73
samba 30, 38, 43, 49, 56, 64,
    65, 84
Santa Catarina 8
São Paulo 7, 11, 13, 20, 29,
    34, 36, 48, 61, 66, 68, 69,
    70, 83
Sarney, José 76
secondary schools 22
Senna, Ayrton 37
Sergipe 7
sertão 7, 20, 21, 29
shantytowns 61
Silva, Maria Auxiliadora 49
slavery 5, 10, 11, 14, 15, 20, 26,
    28, 37, 50, 55, 70, 71
soapstone carvings 33
soccer 36, 43, 66, 67
sugar 10, 13, 18, 19, 26, 40, 50,
    51, 70
sugarcane 7, 10, 18, 19, 40
supernatural 26

telenovela 35
theater 31, 34
Tiradentes 14, 38
Tocantins 8, 9
tourists 82
trade 19, 78, 79

umbanda 26, 27
United States 12, 19, 37, 75,
    76, 77, 78, 79, 80, 81, 82, 83

Vargas, Getúlio 12, 15, 77
Veloso, Caetano 65
Villa-Lobos, Heitor 31
voting 17

women 19, 23, 25, 43, 48, 49,
    53, 55
World Cup 36, 66, 67
World War II 15, 31, 57, 77
writers 5, 22, 72, 73